T0339993

The Courage to Lead through Values

The Courage to Lead through Values

How Management by Values Supports Transformational Leadership, Culture, and Success

Liza-Maria Norlin

A PRODUCTIVITY PRESS BOOK

First published 2021
by Routledge
52 Vanderbilt Avenue, New York, NY 10017

and by Routledge
2 Park Square, Milton Park, Abingdon, Oxon, OX14 4RN

Routledge is an imprint of the Taylor & Francis Group, an informa business

ISBN: 978-0-367-44520-1 (hbk)
ISBN: 978-0-367-44377-1 (pbk)
ISBN: 978-1-003-01015-9 (ebk)

Typeset in Minion Pro
by Deanta Global Publishing Services, Chennai, India

Contents

Forewords

FOREWORD I

I'm not a leader. When I was young, I was shy, groomed to please but lacking the patience to do so. I was impulsive and still am. I had energy and ideas but lacked the charisma to get people on board. At the age of 13 I was asked to lead my Scout group. I led them through mud and rain and we did well but I was their leader by title. I was assigned to them and them to me. A few years later I was named captain of my hockey team but not because of my leadership skills; my wrist shot was deadly and captain I became. As time passed I was able to shake off some of my demons, that kept hindering me from becoming a good leader, while others I couldn't shake off and still to this day, they come back to remind me that leadership is not easy. As an adult I was again given the chance to lead. At times I succeeded but many times I also experienced failures. Leadership, if I can now consider myself to be worthy of the term, did not come easily to me. Still here I am on the front page of this book. Part of me would love to convince you not to keep reading. To simply get you to put this book away and move on to the next one with the photo of a real leader on the cover. I will however not do so. Please keep reading.

As usual it was a very busy afternoon at school. I had anxious parents waiting in the corridor to talk to me, the Vice Principal was in my room helping me solve a problem and I had a message on my phone from the board of education in Sundsvall asking me to call them back right away. Amidst all of this I heard a voice that said: "Hey, I would like to write a book about you". I have to admit that I didn't really know what to make of Liza-Maria Norlin's statement. She was, however, very serious. The journey began with a few simple words. A journey that I many times tried to stop as I didn't really understand why I was chosen for this.

This book is not about how to become a leader. It doesn't provide you with a ten-step programme to turn you from a manager to a leader.

This book is about a very specific conviction that Liza-Maria and I share. Know what you stand for, communicate it, live it and dare to protect it. This is what this book is about. It's about knowing the importance of having the constant courage to find new efficient ways to communicate, discuss, implement and protect at every single level the values and ethos that act as the compass to your organisation.

Leadership was self-imposed as it became a necessity to share the values and ethos that I found myself believing in and wished to spread even more. Barbara Bergström, a real leader, had the courage many years ago to turn beliefs into reality. She wanted children to succeed and soon one school became many. The vision, ethos and values that drove her back then are still the foundation of what we do every single day here at Internationella Engelska Skolan. I understood her vision. I shared her vision and I wanted to bring it to my hometown of Sundsvall, Sweden.

I needed to become a leader if I was to succeed in doing so. It would be a lie to say that the journey was easy. Our school's staff, my colleagues, would most likely agree. They see (and feel) my fumbles, experience my weaknesses and they witness my constant struggles to shake off the demons that have been following me my whole life. Very few, however, would doubt my ability to look forward, to see through the fog and storms and keep the boat sailing forward. They would agree that I share the vision of Barbara Bergström and that I have the guts and courage to implement it. They would probably also say that I have the creativity to find new ways to implement this vision without slowing us down. Most of our thousands of parents could easily tell you what we stand for and the great majority of our students, if not all of them, would say the same. If leadership is about daring to implement a vision and constantly daring to make shared values at the centre of everything you do, then I would, reluctantly, say that I am a leader.

If leadership didn't come easily to me, then success for our school was also not easy. Through the hard work of many great people, such as Petra Håkansson my closest colleague, our school managed to do what many thought impossible. In less than ten years we grew from 250 to 1100 students. We constantly delivered some of the best academic results in our city and managed to be, as per our company's internal surveys, amongst the best schools in our company. Our growth and size did bring debates to our door but even the people driving these debates tend to recognise that we've done something right. This success began with a clear vision of what children need to succeed in life. Liza-Maria chose to use our story to communicate the importance of daring to talk values and thus ensure that everybody walks, together, towards the same goal.

Last, I would like to thank my wonderful family. My wife Jenny, stepson Jonathan and daughter Liv are, more than anybody else, very much aware of my demons but still choose everyday to give me energy to believe in myself despite the many bumps along the road. My hopes are that you'll find joy in seeing that leadership is a journey that doesn't need to be easy but that needs to be guided by a clear understanding of the values that your organisation stands for.

Pascal Brisson
Principal Internationella Engelska Skolan Sundsvall

FOREWORD II

In today's increasingly globalised, chaotic and changing world, the main role of a leader is to develop an organisational culture based on shared values. In my previous work and relevant publications, I have explained why values today represent the DNA of both individual, group and organisational behaviour. Values represent the nucleus of an organisation, the DNA of its culture. All meaning and behaviours orbit around them. If an organisation wishes to use people only as extensions of its machines and technologies, then do not expect them to innovate and become exemplary citizens of your enterprise. At the other extreme, we do not assume organisations will develop cultures of having solely fun; this is a fantasy that no organisation can afford, though work and play are entirely possible and most desirable.

In earlier writings, I have explained the concept of culture reengineering by developing core values that correspond to a configuration of three axes: the economic-pragmatic axis, the ethical-social axis and the emotional-developmental axis. The secret of culture reengineering is to align the core value with the vision and mission of an organisation. To lead the very challenging and complex culture change process—a good transformational leader is needed. Such a leader embeds competencies of coaching, communicating empathy and even spirituality. The extent to which leaders are capable of applying this configuration of values in an organisational context is reflected in the effectiveness of their leadership. As Liza-Maria is proposing in this book, the leader's main task is to develop a culture of shared core values. Values once considered "too soft" to be managed effectively are now accepted as the basis of organisational identity and as a fundamental principle of an organisation's strategy. Cultural models and values are nothing new; they have been studied since the 1970s. However, the perspective of a triaxial model of values, which is the essence of my concept called MBV (managing by values) is new, and more and more companies are now using it to change or sustain their organisational culture.

Visionary leadership entails much more than just directing your followers. It comes from within. Leading from within is a way of guiding yourself towards your inner knowledge and innate strengths. Using your values is the key to uncorking the abundant wellspring within you. I argue, and this book is strengthening the latter, that contemporary leaders need to develop a capacity to embrace and enact on all three axes of values of the proposed triaxial model: economic-pragmatic, ethical-social and emotional-developmental. I wish to label these leaders as "universal" leaders because they deploy and refer to fundamental truths, to worldwide faiths and spiritual traditions that, surprisingly perhaps, share much more in common than may seem to differentiate them.

Leadership today has a direct impact on organisational effectiveness—they provide a platform for aligning the instrumental values. In the short term, organisations and leaders can get by without explicit values; however, in the long term, an absence of values makes the mission nearly impossible. Liza-Maria Norlin's book is a personal account on the great need for leaders to embed values in order to sustain their leadership. The book has been written in a personal tone and reflects the author's personal experience. To the best of my knowledge, it is the first book on this topic written for Swedish readers and the message is straightforward: let's make the concept of MBV known, and let's show that this is not a utopia. As an effective change agent, Liza-Maria provides a wonderful account on the principal elements of MBV which include: the reason why; a crash course on MBV; the role of leaders in changing culture; aligning values to the mission and vision and other related themes. This is a complete manual and a must read for all people who are already in leadership positions or aspire to be. This is not just one more book added to the panoplies of books written about leadership; it is a book that provides the three principle and necessary ingredients for leaders who wish to become effective change agents: a concept (MBV), a methodology and description of some tools. I hope that you will enjoy reading the book and find the content illuminating and useful.

Professor Simon L. Dolan
President of the Global Future of Work Foundation
Email: Simon@globalfutureofwork.com

Preface

Frustration Makes It Happen

Hi!

I'm so happy that you have decided to read this book; my hope is that it will stimulate many thoughts in you. Perhaps you can find some truths or tools but most importantly, I hope you begin to see leadership in a new way. Everything actually began with me being frustrated. If you do nothing about that frustration, it is easy for it to become hopelessness and then nothing constructive or creative occurs. So best to do something about it. In the midst of this frustration, an idea was born that later became so much more than I imagined.

When I told people that I'm writing a book about leadership—as this is how I would summarise the book's contents—I have been met with varied responses. You have perhaps asked the same question: "That's original, doesn't everyone write about leadership?", "Have you had any leadership education?" or even "Oh, how brave!" and "I have to read that". My hope is that the introduction will give you a picture of who I am and why I have written the book. I have chosen to be as present a writer as possible in this book to start a conversation with you. I think that it is through conversation and through building together that we change/develop not only ourselves but also the world.

After more than 20 years of being a teacher and politically active, it's probably quite natural that I suffer from frustration. In the last few years, there have been two questions in particular that I have spent a lot of time and thought on. One is the increasing mental ill health amongst young people and women. As a local politician I tangibly see how the number of people on sick leave has reached completely unreasonable levels and continues to rise in our important institutions such as schools, healthcare and social services. This is an unbelievably difficult situation, in many countries, not only for the individual but also for welfare and society at large. The other question is about school. New suggestions for solutions replace each other at the same time as way too many youths don't achieve passing grades, insecurity rises and we stand on the brink of a growing teacher shortage. Although I'm painting quite a depressing picture, there is, of course, so much good to talk about, but these are possibly our generation's most important challenges. My frustration doesn't actually come from the challenges themselves but from the debate about them and the solutions presented. I realise that even I can be a part of this. Don't worry now, this will not be a political book and it isn't something that just applies to the public sector either, but it gives a picture of where this book started out.

It feels like something has gone wrong somewhere. Now and then we talk about how managers are important, sometimes it is middle management's fault, and sometimes we name a lack of leadership. However, I seldom hear about what is wrong with the leadership and how it should change. Do you recognise: "The political leadership has failed", "Teachers must be more authoritarian", "Middle management are not loyal to the leadership" and so on? My question is: Is there a kind of leadership that can stand the test of time? A leadership that gives customers, students, users what they expect and need, while at the same time allowing the staff to thrive?

The search for the answer gave me the idea to tell a story worth telling. Sometimes you don't have to look far, sometimes the answer is just around the corner. A few years ago, I was in the audience of a seminar at a conference. It was about how a school works with values to begin with. I personally call myself a real "values nerd" but it hit me how concretely they worked with anchoring the school's values in both the big and the small. If you live in Sundsvall, Sweden, as I do, it is impossible to ignore this school, it is talked about everywhere. I understood in the seminar that the great results were not due to coincidence or happy circumstances. In Chapter 2 you will read more facts about the school. Today, when the school has existed for ten years, there is definitely a story to tell. Actually, regardless of whether you know the school or not, and regardless of your opinion on the school, it is unique in many ways and I am convinced that this has a lot to do with the leadership.

One day I bumped into the school's principal, Pascal Brisson. We said hello as we knew each other from before. After saying hello, I said: "Hey, I would like to write a book about you". He laughed and I understood that he didn't really take me seriously. So, I added: "Well, it's true, for real!". We didn't have time to say so much more about that then and there but some days later, he contacted me and asked what I meant. One evening, a couple of months later, we met and I told him about all my ideas and thoughts and said that I would like to connect them with his journey and the leadership he represents. I don't know if he was easily convinced, it's not every day that someone wants to write a book about you. It became clear quite early on that it was a big step for him to let go of the control of something, and in this case to another person to write about him and an institution he cared a lot about. But it was a yes. Since that day ideas about the book have developed from our discussions and various interviews. I see it as a great privilege to be able to do this, and I am so thankful for his trust. It is an important story, interesting in many ways, and a central feature in discussions about leadership.

But it isn't leadership in general that interests me, but when leadership is clearly linked to values. It's specifically that that made Pascal interesting for me, even if he himself doesn't always agree with me and my analyses of him and his leadership and this clear connection to values. When he reads this book himself, perhaps he will see his leadership in a different way.

The next step was to deepen my understanding of leadership theory. What can I find about values-driven leadership or values-based leadership? Not so much in Sweden I found, so I expanded my search to outside of Sweden's borders. In the end, I found an article written by some researchers: "Management by Values (MBV): A New Philosophy for a New Economic Order",[1] which presented a leadership that they found was what was required to meet the complexity that is the face of our world today. This article got me to read a book called *Managing by Values*.[2] It's a guide, you could say, to doing what the subtitle says: "A Corporate Guide to Living, Being Alive, and Making a Living in the 21st Century". I don't know if you have ever got the feeling of some kind of total affinity, as if someone understands exactly what you think and feel. It was a bit like that for me when I read the book. That it has been researched for over 30 years and that there is a method that can explain what I am thinking. After reading the book and after some interviews with Pascal, I realised even more how these theories and methods coincide with the leadership Pascal represents in an incredible way. To bring together a methodology with a real example that has their processes completely separated from each other became an exciting journey. It is this journey that you will get to participate in when you read this book. On a personal level it has been extremely exciting and self improving to combine knowledge of sustainable organisations, culture transformation and of values' central meaning with an example from a school's journey in Sweden. My hope is that the practical example together with the theory will bring forward the vision of leadership in Sweden and in your own country. There needs to be a "leadership movement" to lead us, our organisations, institutions and businesses forward in an increasingly complex world.

Hopefully this book will make a difference for you, your workplace, your company or organisation and perhaps the country's development. Nothing is impossible! It starts with you and me.

Partway through the process I decided to contact Simon L. Dolan,[3] the person who personifies Management by Values. This was partly because of a worry that made me send him an email. Since I realised I wanted to use a lot of what he had written, I wanted to inform him of that, so he wouldn't be angry that I had stolen his ideas, you never know. Instead of protectionism, I met a missionary, a person driven to change the world. Or as he said in the first Skype conversation: "As teacher and politician you are a change agent". Which he also used as an epithet to describe himself later on in the conversation. I believe that Pascal Brisson with his team are change agents in one of Sweden's most regulated and important institutions—school. This book gives you the possibility of meeting three different "change agents" from different contexts and at the same time give you tools to create what Dolan would call a cultural transformation.

Liza-Maria Norlin

NOTES

1. Dolan, S. L.and Richely, B. A. (2006). Management by values (MBV): A new philosophy for a new economic order. *Handbook of Business Strategy*, Vol. 7 No. 1, pp. 235–238. https://doi.org/10.1108/10775730610618873. Emerald Group Publishing. http://www.emeraldinsight.com/doi/abs/10.1108/10775730610618873 (15 January 2017).
2. Dolan, S. L., Garcia, S. and Richely, B. (2006). *Managing by Values, A Corporate Guide to Living, Being Alive, and Making a Living in the 21st Century*. London: Palgrave Macmillan.
3. Professor Simon L. Dolan, ESADE Future of Work Chair and President of the Global Future of Work. Foundation Email: Simon@globalfutureofwork.com.

Acknowledgements

Thanks to my husband Thomas and our patient and loving daughters Adelina and Timea, and to all my friends out there; this could not have happened without you. Creation happens together with others!

I would also like to thank with all my heart professor and change agent Simon L. Dolan, Principal Pascal Brisson and the people at Internationella Engelska Skolan Sundsvall (IESS) and Internationella Engelska Skolan (IES) who have contributed enormously to this book.

- Allanius, Anna-Maria—From Fall 2017, vice principal IESS
- Beranger, Jocelyn—Teacher IESS
- Bergström, Barbara—Founder IES
- Brisson, Pascal—Principal IESS
- Challis, Marjorie—Teacher IESS
- Dolan, Simon L.—Professor, President of The Global Future of Work Foundation www.simondolan.com
- Hall, Jens—Teacher IESS
- Henriksson, Karin—Receptionist IESS
- Håkansson, Petra—Vice principal IESS
- Nilsson, Mattias—Teacher IESS
- Pousette, Gustaf—Teacher IESS (Named by those who were interviewed in the book)
- Riber, Ralph—CEO Internationella Engelska Skolan, 2013–2017
- Strijdom, Pieter—Head of Student Development Team IESS
- Åkerström, Kim—Previous student, IESS years 6 to 9
- Translation: Marjorie Challis, 2018
- Cover design and photography: © 2020 Per Helander

Liza-Maria

About the Author

 **Liza-Maria Norlin** is currently a project and process director at Bron Innovation and politician for the Christian Democrats (KD). She served as a member of KD's party board from 2007 to 2009, and has been a regular member since 2017. In addition, since 2014, she has served as a group leader in KD Sundsvall and a member of the municipal council in Sundsvall. In 2019, she appeared as a third name on KD's EU electoral ballot in the European Parliament elections. Previously, she served as a Member of the Swedish Parliament from 2009 to 2010 and chair of the Christian Democrats Sundsvall. She has a degree of Master of Education for the Upper Secondary School and has taught high school students Swedish and English for many years. She graduated in 2003 from Mid Sweden University in Härnösand. She can be contacted through www. lizamarianorlin.com.

I love values as they have been very formative throughout my life. In the way I was brought up and taught how to view the world and people; in my education as I got to experience many different schools in Sweden and Europe; at university as I studied language and literature; as a teacher when wanting to motivate, teach and support young people; as a politician on local, regional and national level; and perhaps most importantly as a parent and in relationships with other people.

My values over the past few years have made me experience a sense of frustration and now I have decided to do something about it. Join me in a conversation together with Principal Pascal Brisson and Managing by Values!

1

Everything Has a Beginning

In the beginning, you act like a leader — until one day you realise that you have become one.

Pascal Brisson

Pascal Brisson, high school teacher, sees the advertisement in the paper "Internationella Engelska Skolan wants to open in Sundsvall, Sweden". Something in the advertisement piques his interest, it stimulates his personal drive, creativity and willingness to take risks for the potential of fixing something that isn't working. In December 2008, he emails the CEO of Internationella Engelska Skolan and says he is interested in the job as principal of a new school in Sundsvall. "It was clear that I would get the job when during an interview I said: 'One thing I guarantee you, I can really say to all parents and staff that I stand for your values.'"

Today, a little more than 11 years later, I am sitting in front of a principal and leader who feels confident and sure in his role. In Sundsvall, his is a well-known name and within the school group Internationella Engelska Skolan he is a very appreciated leader. In ten years the school in Sundsvall has gone from zero students and no staff to 1100 students and 125 staff. If you read Pascal's welcome on the website, it's there in the first sentence: "Internationella Engelska Skolan Sundsvall is in constant evolution".[1] It is physically clear when you visit the school—a new parkour park is in place while at the same time expansion and rebuilding continue. It is a result of how the school has constantly grown and continues to grow. I still get the feeling that this constant evolution is more than just the physical environment and that the school grows in numbers. What does this constant evolution mean for Pascal?

A drive that never stands still, it is a part of my personality, constantly in motion, I constantly look at our organisation, what works, what isn't working so well? But at the same time as we grow and constantly develop our routines, the foundation has never changed.

Into the room walks Pieter Strijdom, the school's Head of Student Development Team (responsible for helping students to feel safe). He is one of the people who has been there since the beginning and it is clear that he and Pascal are close. I take the opportunity of course to ask if it is true that the school is in some state of constant evolution, where the answer with a big smile and perhaps a little sigh is: "Oooo yes!"

The email that Pascal sent to the CEO resulted in an interview opportunity, the possibility to meet other principals from other parts of Sweden and some visits to other schools within the school group Internationella Engelska Skolan. When Pascal met the founder of Internationella Engelska Skolan, Barbara Bergström, and even the principal in Enskede, Robert Clark, there was a feeling that gave the strongest of impressions. A feeling of being at home. This feeling arose both because of shared values and small details. One thing that really irritated Pascal in his time as a high school teacher was that students didn't come on time to lessons. He considers not coming on time to be a practical detail that has practical consequences (disturbs others, causes explanations to be missed, etc.) and a result of poor values; a lack of respect.

I liked that IES had high expectations on students and they both pushed and supported them. The school's leadership also explained why they worked in the way they did and do. I felt that out of that foundation that was already there in values and behaviour, I could build a school I could believe in

says Pascal.

Pascal describes himself as a confident person who loves to take risks and likes challenges but at the same time is very paranoid. I understand through our conversations that Pascal really analyses his personal characteristics and sees both the positive and negative consequences in these. To dare to take the step of building a school from the ground up requires courage to take risks, therefore, he saw this as a perfect challenge. In the beginning the paranoia led to the motivation to read everything he could about the school. It wasn't all the lovely formulations on websites or the excellent results that you could read on Skolverket's (Swedish National Agency for Education) website that convinced him. An important reason was the founder herself, Barbara, and her values. There was a clear picture of what she wanted to create.

> Barbara Bergström has from the beginning had a clear picture of what she wants, she knew what she wanted to create when she began. She has met a lot of resistance and has never given up. For us principals and for leaders, many trends come and go, it is important to keep to what you believe in, regardless of being pushed in different directions. This is a very important part of how to succeed and Barbara has really shown that it works and is a role model. You have to keep focus in spite of pressure from outside

says Pascal in a way that clearly shows his respect and admiration for Barbara.

In addition to the personal characteristics he names in describing himself I would add humour and self awareness that has come through in our conversations, an example being from Pascal's first job interview for the position of principal.

> I sat and waited before my interview when a man came and sat next to me. I later found out it was Barbara's husband. We sat and talked for nearly 45 minutes. Then I went in. The interview went on with the CEO and vice CEO. At one point Barbara comes into the room and says hi and talks briefly. Then she asked what job I was there for: 'Principal or vice principal?' I smiled and pointed to the CEO and said 'I'm here for his job.' Everyone laughed (except for the CEO who is no longer a part of the company anymore). Yes, I'm that kind of person and I think Barbara liked that

Pascal says and laughs.

I ask Barbara Bergström if she remembers the first time she met Pascal, and she does, very well.

> The first time I met Pascal was the 27th of November 2008. I remember exactly where in the audience he sat, and he surely does too. He looked at me hard the whole time. When we later spoke with each other we both realised that we had a lot in common.

Pascal Brisson was born and raised in Embrun, Ontario which is a small town in Canada. He grew up in what he himself calls a school environment.

His father was chairman of the school board, his mother was a teacher and in his family there were many teachers and principals. This has made him feel at home in the school environment and consequently be attracted to it. One of his dreams has always been to build and start his own school. One day he got the chance and of course took it.

"How many teachers get the chance to start a completely new school?" was the answer when I wondered why he chose to take on the great responsibility of being a principal in a new school.

My question in response was if it was still an obvious choice to become principal. I describe the principal's job as tough in many ways, as principal, you are liable. There are many principals who can't handle the workload, the pay isn't especially good and there is a lot of pressure from different directions, so why would he want to be a principal?

> I didn't really think of it that way. I saw the creativity in building something, it's the creating part and starting something new that inspires me. In my case it is about a really good school. An opportunity to meet my need to fix things I think are wrong. This is something I get to work with every day and it makes me feel good. Then of course when I did stand there—a principal, that was me—nothing was yet in place and at the same time I could see that schooling is the most regulated area in Sweden, I could feel the panic.

The time between the email and interviews until Pascal became principal was quite a quick process. In the beginning it was mostly interest and curiosity around applying for the job and it wasn't an instant "Yes!" when Barbara called some days before Christmas and said: "Mr Brisson I have the pleasure of offering you the job".

"It wasn't appreciated when I said: 'I will think about it', I heard.

"Why didn't you say yes? Weren't you quite convinced?"

> Have to ask my wife first so I don't say yes to something completely crazy! I had a job anyway. Later during Christmas break I said yes to the job. In two weeks I went from a teacher in a large high school to the Principal of nothing.

Suddenly Pascal had the task of recruiting staff from abroad and Sweden to a school that didn't exist yet. Something that stands out in the school in Sundsvall, is that many of the staff are from Canada, a choice Pascal has made. This is why he goes there to recruit the right people and convince them to move to Sweden and Sundsvall. He was at home in Sundsvall again after Christmas break and it was time to organise an open house in Tonhallen (a concert theatre) to attract students and parents to a school that didn't have any teachers or other staff.

"A school can't exist without students!" said Pascal.

Up until the month of June, there were two people who would organise everything that was needed for school start in August. One challenge in this situation was just to "sell" something that you couldn't touch or visit. Pascal chose, together with one of the first recruits, Jens Hall, to call around to parents in Sundsvall and tell them about the school.

"I'm not at all a salesman so this wasn't an easy task, but in some way we needed to reach out and talk about what our future school could offer parents and their children. It was just to do it".

When everything goes very quickly and there is a lot of practical things that must be organised, it's easy to focus on the practical, and difficult to find time to engage in the question of why one does something. To be able to anchor the values or principles behind everything that has to be done can feel burdensome. When you visit Internationella Engelska Skolan Sundsvall (IESS) today, you get the understanding that nothing is random, it seems as if thought has gone into everything.

One evening before the school started, Petra Håkansson (Vice Principal today) and Jens Hall (Head of Swedish as a second language and teacher) met at my place. We conversed and discussed what would be important starting points for the school. The group, Internationella Engelska Skolan, already has clear principles, but we still wanted to think about what they mean for us and formulate our own interpretations. What does it mean to feel safe, to have an international stamp and to see students as individuals? That evening we wrote a mission statement. We had a huge mission for our school in Sundsvall. What we wanted to deliver was: 1. A safe and orderly work environment with "tough love", and poor conduct has consequences and not punishment; 2. High expectations both socially and academically; and 3. That students have command of the English language. Then there are values behind this that help us to reach these three expectations, such as to celebrate success, have fun together, happiness, dare to be "crazy", try to see things from the child's perspective. This is what we want to deliver together with our values and to create in turn the culture we have at school

Pascal says.

During that evening, one of the conclusions drawn was that at the school in Sundsvall, every individual will be seen. It sounds like something one has heard before and is understood in many situations as obvious. But what makes it actually happen is that it isn't just something described as important but it is also connected to actions. For the staff it is about the leaders constantly working so that the right person is in the right place and does the right thing based on who that person is. This of course creates the best possible result for the school and also the work situation for employees where they feel seen and where they can do their best no matter who they are. To see every person can also imply that they come to the conclusion that the right place for the person is not this workplace.

> We leaders coach staff at the school to work from our concept so they can participate and help to deliver what we have promised our students and parents. It sometimes happens, after a time of coaching, that the teacher or we leaders feel that it doesn't work and then we have a conversation about that. We usually come to an agreement that we will go our separate ways. This is a way to see the importance of the individual in a larger system. So that every student can be seen as an individual at IESS, the leadership works with teachers to give them the knowledge, tools and conditions that are needed to be able to see the student.

For me, who has followed the school debate for many years, where amongst other things the size of the class has regularly come into the discussion, I can feel some doubt about whether it is possible to see every student, particularly in a school with classes that have 32 students. In the conversation with Pascal, I have understood that this is one of the questions and reflections he often gets from different places. This subject requires almost a whole chapter and of course discussion with both students and teachers; that is why I will come to this question later on. In short, it depends on how a system is in line with values and goal setting.

In August 2009, the doors of Internationella Engelska Skolan Sundsvall opened. Two hundred fifty students in years 6–9 were welcomed by 25 teachers in the newly renovated 100-year-old building featuring English Oxford-like architecture.

NOTE

1. Internationella Engelska Skolan Sundsvall. Welcome from the Principal. https://sundsvall.engelska.se/about-our-school/welcome-principal (14 March 2017).

2

A Story That Needed to Be Told

If you want to move people, it has to be toward a vision that is positive for them, that taps important values, that gets them something they desire, it has to be presented in a compelling way, that they feel inspired to follow.

Martin Luther King, Jr

During my interviews with the principal of Internationella Engelska Skolan Sundsvall (IESS), Pascal Brisson, one recurring theme is the upcoming inspection made by the Skolinspektion (Swedish government body that is responsible for the quality of schooling in Sweden by way of regularly inspecting schools and giving feedback on how they can improve). This is not something one takes lightly and now the school had to prove whether it was upholding the quality they so actively worked for. See Figure 2.1.

In the middle of May, I meet a relieved and extremely happy Mr Brisson.

"We have got our answer from Skolinspektionen!"

When he explains Skolinspektionen's decision, I understand how much he cares about the school and that he is happy to get to tell his staff how their hard work can now be celebrated.

"We passed without any corrections, we fulfil expectations in all areas!" Pascal says and breathes out with a satisfied expression.

Even though I have dreamt of being a writer since I was little and I remember how in school I wrote through notebook after notebook, my goal in this project wasn't to write a book. There are stories to tell. A lot of the information swishes by on social media or newsfeeds but all too rarely we get to hear the story behind the event, a person or operation. In a time when society is becoming more and more complex, where expectations in many contexts increase, where effectivity, quality and renewal is expected for survival, that's where leadership becomes more important than ever.

Beslut 2017-05-12 Dnr 44-2016:11084
Skolinspektionen,
Box 23069, 104 35 Stockholm, Besöksadress: Sveavägen 159

Skolinspektionen avslutar härmed tillsynen i Internationella Engelska Skolan i Sundsvall

Bedömning
Det har vid tillsynen inte framkommit annat än att skolenheten uppfyller författningarnas krav inom de arbetsområden som granskats.

Områden där Skolinspektionen inte har funnit brister:

- Undervisning och lärande. Internationella Engelska Skolan i Sverige AB uppfyller författningarnas krav inom undervisning och lärande.

- Trygghet, studiero och åtgärder mot kränkande behandling. Internationella Engelska Skolan i Sverige AB uppfyller författningarnas krav inom trygghet, studiero och åtgärder mot kränkande behandling.

- Styrning och utveckling av verksamheten. Internationella Engelska Skolan i Sverige AB uppfyller författningarnas krav inom styrning och utveckling av verksamheten.

FIGURE 2.1
Decision on the 12th of May, 2017, by Skolinspektionen after inspecting Internationella Engelska Skolan Sundsvall. In all areas of teaching, calm study environment and actions to take against bullying and management and development of the organisation, Sundsvall had no issues. It was like getting 100% on an exam.

As a teacher I have somehow always strived to be that teacher that I saw growing up in American movies. That person who enchants students and changes their destiny. A naïve wish and an apparently unreachable goal, but it has motivated and driven me in my role as teacher. Hand on heart, isn't that what should characterise the best possible school? A school where all students love to be, where all students with their different and unique backgrounds can develop and reach undreamed-of heights both as people and in final school results? If that isn't the goal, what should we aim for? My experience however says that it isn't goals that are missing in our Swedish schools. There's no one who wants to be "Sweden's worst school" or who wants students to fail, or that children and young people graduate one day and say "These were the worst years of my life". As active participants in the public debate and political decision making both at a national level and municipal level, it appears that Swedish school management has been characterised for the most part by goal setting and in the worst case micromanagement.

The school is an example of what one can call a complex organisation and through our time's fast development more and more organisations/companies/operations become complex. This is why a school is a good starting point from where to understand the leadership that is needed today. What is meant by a complex organisation then? Sören Augustinsson, Doctor of Philosophy in work science and university lecturer at Kristianstad's College, and Ulf Ericsson, Doctor of Philosophy of Industrial Work Science and university lecturer in psychology with a focus on working life and learning at the University of Kristianstad, wrote an article in the paper about complex operations: "More Complex with Complexity".[1] They describe complex operations:

> A clear sign that your operation is complex, or not, is if it is possible to say in advance and with certainty predict and control what is going to happen in detail [and] long term. If you can predict what is going to happen in detail and in the long term then the operation is not complex.

A school is the perfect example of a complex operation. Here simple or quick solutions or models don't work, but as Augustinsson and Ericsson express in the article: "Remember that complexity must be met with complexity!" There's a school near me that shows that it's possible to deliver quality, results and satisfied students, parents and staff, during a period of fast expansion. I would say it is one of Sweden's best schools and I will soon explain why. There is of course no such thing as a perfect school or operation, but there are definitely examples that show that it is possible to have long-term sustainable organisations that live up to their goals.

Since the PISA[2] report in 2012, headlines about the school crisis have been dominating the education world. They write about lack of respect, need for more order and that parents need to be more involved. We read about increasing segregation, about youths who have bad habits and teachers with terrible working conditions. The list is long and reports show that results become worse at the same time as teachers struggle in their work situation. At the same time, we read about all the fantastic things that happen in our schools. We have all met the engaged teacher and seen survey results that show satisfied students and parents. In the 2015/2016 school year, there were more than 985,000 elementary students at school in Sweden.

If you are in Sundsvall, Sweden and mention Engelska Skolan, everyone has heard about the school, many have their children there and even more have placed their children on the waiting list to eventually have their child get their education from there. Some say that the successes are because it is a non-government school and with that comes advantages and others say it's the "English discipline" that is the key. I think it is more complex and at the same time more basic than that. Whatever the reason or what you think of the school, I see it as important to talk about the leadership that characterises and has characterised the school from the start. What lies behind my statement that Internationella Engelska Skolan Sundsvall is one of Sweden's best schools? The school is successful in basically all areas a school should be successful in. I'd like to take a moment to present the statistics, results and reports about the school and how it looks compared to other schools. Of course, there are children, parents, staff and others who don't agree with my statement; it has of course happened that mistakes have been made and actions have been in error. But the statistics show that this school does something that leads to extremely positive effects for the school as an educational institution and workplace.

In August 2009, Internationella Engelska Skolan Sundsvall opened their doors to 250 students from years 6 to 9 and 25 employees. The school is a part of the concern Internationella Engelska Skolan[3] (IES) that Mrs Barbara Bergström founded in 1993 to give students the opportunity to choose a school where they can learn to command the English language in a calm and safe environment with high academic expectations. From a national perspective, the school group Internationella Engelska Skolan has had a large increase in the number of students since 2009. There were 34 schools around Sweden in 2017. This is still just a small part of Sweden's 1,023,970[4] elementary school students who go to these schools, approximately 22,000 children and teenagers. See Figure 2.2.

Internationella Engelska Skolan chooses to publicise their academic results clearly on their website. They see good results as the reason for their growth. Statistics from Skolverket regarding students' results in the national tests in year 9 (2016) show that their schools stand out in comparison to others in the subjects of mathematics, Swedish and English. National tests are standardised tests that all students in Sweden complete in year 3 (in Swedish and mathematics), year 6 (in English, Swedish and mathematics) and year 9 (in English, Swedish, mathematics, science and social studies) and again at non-compulsory high school level if they continue. In Figure 2.3, the percentage of students who have achieved final grades of A to C is compared to the grades in the national test in year 9 (2016).[5]

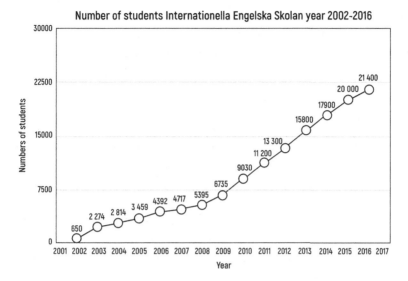

FIGURE 2.2
The increase in the number of students in the school group Internationella Engelska Skolan from 2002 to 2017. (Source: Internationella Engelska Skolan's website. Internationella Engelska Skolan. Results. https://engelska.se/sv/about-ies/results (22 May 2017).)

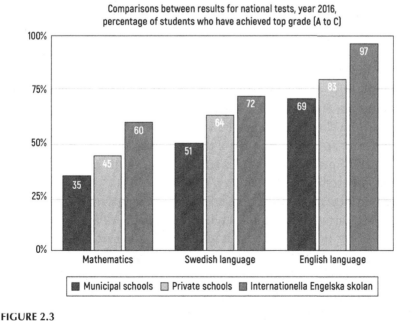

FIGURE 2.3
Percentage of students who have achieved grades A to C in the national tests in year 9 (2016). A comparison between the average in municipal schools, private schools and Internationella Engelska Skolan. Private schools referred to in the diagram are publicly funded independent schools.

With quite a limited number of Sweden's total elementary school students, you could argue that the good results are possible because of the kinds of students who go to their schools. This analysis requires its own book but one way they answer this question is to measure what they call "added value"[6] for their students. They measure how the school has succeeded in helping students improve their results over a three-year period. A figure that many school researchers recommend looking at, that is, students' development over time. It is now possible for a school to compare students' results on the national tests in year 6 with the results in year 9. An example of this is that if you compare IES and government schools' results in the national test in mathematics in year 6, the difference is 11%. Three years later in the national test in mathematics in year 9, the difference is 29%; this can be described as an "added value" of 18% (the difference between 29% and 11%). This shows how IES succeeds in improving students' academic success over a three-year period.

This chapter gives you a description of why I have chosen to look at the leadership of a specific school in Sweden. If you want more statistics or information about IES, go to their website: www.engelska.se or www.skolverket.se and www.skolinspektion.se. I have stated here that Internationella Engelska Skolan Sundsvall is Sweden's best school so I would therefore like to present facts specifically about that school. A successful, or call it a well-working, school will deliver good results in teaching and learning, feeling safe, calm learning environment and actions against offensive treatment and in the governance and development of the institution. Staff, teachers, students and parents—everyone needs to be asked from their perspective how well they feel the school works in these different areas. It is because of their feedback on all these areas and from different perspectives that makes Internationella Engelska Skolan Sundsvall interesting.

Here are a lot of results from the Skolinspektion, school survey of Autumn 2016.[7] We'll start with year 5 and students' answers. See Figure 2.4.

In the chart in Figure 2.5, it is possible to compare Internationella Engelska Skolan Sundsvall's results with Internationella Engelska Skolan Sweden's results and with those of all participating schools. IES in Sundsvall has the best results in all points except for the first. To clarify, next to the minus marked points, where a negative statement was used, Skolverket has recalculated results so high numbers are positive. From this book's perspective, it is especially interesting to note where the differences

FIGURE 2.4
Photograph of several of Skolinspektion's surveys from 2016. Photo: Norlins förlag.

are largest in comparison to other schools and they include 11. In my school we respect each other; 14. In my school students follow the rules of conduct; 16. I have a calm learning environment during lessons; 20. I feel safe at school; 21. Adults at school react if they notice that someone has been mean to a student. See Figure 2.5.

Let us now look at results from students in year 9 during the same period. If we look at the bars, we can see bigger differences in comparison to Internationella Engelska Skolan as a whole and with the other schools that have participated in the survey. All the bars give the school in Sundsvall the highest result. It is clear that even from students in year 9 that questions about a calm learning environment, safety, basic values and hindrance of offensive behaviour and bullying is where the differences are reported as greatest. See Figure 2.6.

What do parents who have their children and teenagers at the school think then? The chart in Figure·2.7 shows that even when you ask guardians, the Internationella Engelska Skolan Sundsvall stands out in a positive way. The bars connected to a calm learning environment are those that show the biggest difference compared to the other schools: 8.6 versus 6.5. The school gets the highest score for safety and hindrance of offensive behaviour and bullying; they get a score of 9.4 out of a possible 10.

The employees are of course central for an organisation, company or school to be successful. From a societal perspective, as I also briefly

Survey responses year 5
Skolenkäten autumn 2016, Skolinspektionen

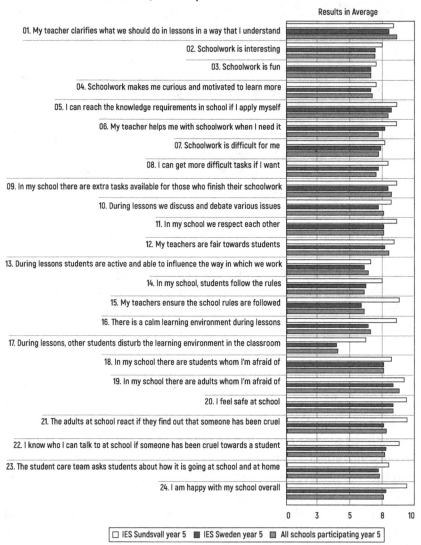

FIGURE 2.5
The results from the survey of year 5 (2016) where they compare Internationella Engelska Skolan Sundsvall's results with Internationella Engelska Skolan Sweden and with all participating schools. The white bars show that IES Sundsvall has the highest results in all areas.

Survey responses year 9
Skolenkäten autumn 2016, Skolinspektionen

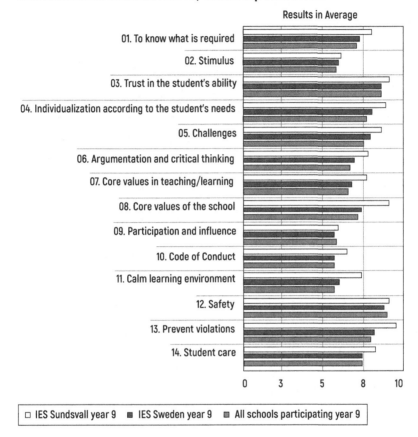

FIGURE 2.6
The results from the survey of year 9 (2016). The biggest area where IES Sundsvall stands out is on Point 08 about basic values in teaching and learning.

discussed in my introduction, employees' health within the school and the possibility of future recruitment to the profession, their answers are extremely central to judging an organisation's success. Let us therefore also look at employee-related results from the survey. See Figure 2.7.

This is the chart that shows the biggest differences in comparison to the other schools that participated in the investigation. If we are to give our children the best education, we need to guarantee the right work environment for teachers, the pedagogical employees. The biggest difference can be seen regarding routines, a difference of a whole 2.7

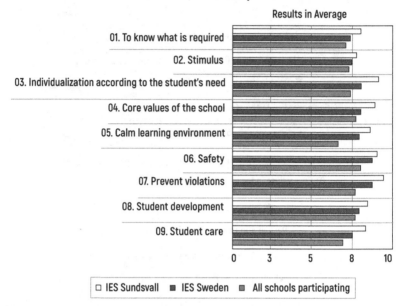

Survey responses guardians
Skolenkäten autumn 2016, Skolinspektionen

Results in Average

01. To know what is required
02. Stimulus
03. Individualization according to the student's need
04. Core values of the school
05. Calm learning environment
06. Safety
07. Prevent violations
08. Student development
09. Student care

0   3   5   8   10

☐ IES Sundsvall   ■ IES Sweden   ▣ All schools participating

FIGURE 2.7
The results from the survey of guardians where they compare Internationella Engelska Skolan's results in Sundsvall with Internationella Engelska Skolan Sweden and with all participating schools. Internationella Engelska Skolan Sundsvall has the highest results in all areas.

points. Then comes professional development with a difference of 2.6 points. The pedagogical leadership is also a clear marker, Engelska Skolan Sundsvall gets 9.7 out of 10, in comparison to other schools that get 7.4. A calm learning environment also gets a high score, 9.1 in comparison to Internationella Engelska Skolan's 6.8. See Figure 2.8.

As a basis for the different points in each chart are a number of questions that students, guardians and pedagogical staff members have answered. If you are interested, more information can be found in Skolverket's reports.

There are of course many reasons why the results look the way they do. I have chosen to talk about the school's journey from the start to present day from a leadership perspective where values are fundamental. A story that is worth telling can of course be told in many different ways; this is my way.

Survey responses educational staff
Skolenkäten autumn 2016, Skolinspektionen

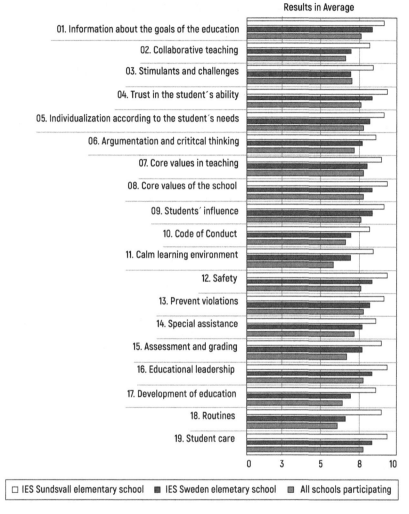

FIGURE 2.8
Results from the survey on pedagogical staff (2016) where they compare Internationella Engelska Skolan's results in Sundsvall with Internationella Engelska Skolan Sweden and with all the participating schools. Internationella Engelska Skolan Sundsvall has the highest results in all areas.

NOTES

1. Augustinsson, S. and Ericsson, U. (19 April 2013). Mer komplext med komplexitet. *Tidningen Chef.* http://chefstidningen.se/reportage/mer-komplext-med-komplexi tet (18 May 2017).
2. PISA (Programme for International Student Assessment) is the world's largest student study and is an OECD project. Both OECD and non-OECD countries participate in the study. It looks at abilities in mathematics, science and reading comprehension. https://www.skolverket.se/statistik-och-utvardering/internationel la-studier/pisa (05 September 2017).
3. Internationella Engelska Skolan. Founder's introduction. https://engelska.se/about -ies/founder's-introduction (22 May 2017).
4. Skolverket. Quick facts. https://www.skolverket.se/statistik-och-utvardering/sta tistik-i-tabeller/snabbfakta-1.120821 (22 May 2017).
5. Internationella Engelska Skolan. National test results released for 2016: Strong results show value added for Internationella Engelska Skolan students between years 6 and 9. https://engelska.se/news/national-test-results-released-2016-strong-results-show-value-added-internationella-engelska (22 May 2017).
6. Internationella Engelska Skolan. Added value. https://engelska.se/news/national-test-results-released-2016-strong-results-show-value-added-internationella-engelska (22 May 2017).
7. Skolinspektionen. Siris Kvalitet och resultat i skolan. http://siris.skolverket.se/sir is/ris.skolenkat.search?p_termin=%25&p_kommun=2281&p_foretag=%25&p_lan dsting=%25&p_enhet=54802332&p_typ=%25&p_back_url=http%3A%2F%2Fsir is.skolverket.se%2Fsiris%2Fris.skolenkat.searchform%3Fp_kommun%3D2281% 26p_foretag%3D%2525%26p_landsting%3D%2525%26p_enhet%3D54802332%26 p_typ%3D%2525%26p_termin%3D%2525 (22 May 2017).

3

Crash Course MBV

Instructions are management tools of "bosses" and objectives are those of administrators. Leaders use values.[1]

S. Dolan, S. Garcia, B. Richley

In 1989, when the Berlin Wall fell, his thoughts went to how the West and East could join to build a community together. It caused him to start working with values in organisations. He is a pacifist and his mission is to change the world. Born in Israel and it is there and in America that he has studied. He took his PhD at the University of Minnesota, where his area of study was organisational psychology, behavioural science and administration. Today he is responsible for Future Work through ESADE, one of the world's leading business schools in Barcelona. Before that, he taught for over 25 years at the University of Montreal and McGill in Canada. He has written more than 55 books now translated into many languages and has held more than 600 lectures, seminars and workshops all over the world. In addition, he has mastered seven languages. This is Simon L. Dolan and he has quite simply a CV beyond the ordinary.

I knew that I wanted to write a book about values and their importance for long-term sustainable leadership. It was just that which I recognised in Principal Pascal Brisson and Internationella Engelska Skolan Sundsvall. In the search for research and literature, I found an article that later led me to the book *Managing by Values.*[2] To read it was to really put words to the type of leadership I wanted to talk about.

Different times and different societies have affected the type of leadership, control and management required. The question becomes what kind of leadership is required in a time where technology is developing faster all the time. In a time of globalisation and communication without borders; in a time where new threats and fears take root; in a time when we don't know what we should educate our youth in as we don't know the jobs of the future; and in a time that is first and foremost characterised by constant change.

In the 1970s at the University of Minnesota, Simon L. Dolan was almost done with his PhD studies when he was hit by what he called a "management reality shock".[3] He was then a research assistant at the Mayo Clinic and studied patients who had survived their first heart attack. He discovered that 90% of these patients felt that their stress was work related. In companies and organisations, he saw a constant progress towards greater pressure on managers to raise productivity rather than reflect on questions like: Why are we doing this? And what is the purpose of the organisation? The observations and experiences led to him beginning to study work-related stress, the seeds that later became the management and leadership model Management by Values (MBV).

Throughout this book, you will get a greater understanding of this model but in this chapter, you will get a brief introduction. MBV is useful on many different levels but for leadership, you can say the purpose is threefold: To *simplify*, *guide* and *secure commitment*. Different times and societies require different leadership or management models. Since organisations have become more complex; met an increased trend of independence and responsibility; methods in employment are characterised by greater cooperation; network and flat organisations grow; and where managers are expected to be more than just leaders and facilitators—yes, in this time there is a new management model taking form.

Technological advancements in agriculture and the increasing productivity of the early 20th century meant that more workers became available for other things and this in turn made it possible for modern industry to grow.[4] People moved to cities and a new consumer society grew. The first half of the 20th century was characterised by mass production and the assembly line principle. Management and leadership in the workforce were first and foremost characterised by management by instructions (MBI), that is, that instructions and information to the workers should be clear so that every worker knows their job. The purpose[5] of the organisations was to produce products for a tangible and stable market. Management was characterised by the "top-down" principle and subordination and control over the level of activity to achieve the goal.

Since the market, workforce and tasks have changed, there is also a need to increase flexibility in the system and the potential to motivate workers. The Second World War left behind a new Europe with new possibilities and challenges. For Sweden, the export industry peaked, until approximately 1960: "The period 1950–70 is usually seen as a golden age of growth, where the industrial society's development culminated and consumption and production more than doubled".[6] At the same time, we saw a new sector grow, the service sector. One of the reasons for this in Sweden was "the Swedish model" that was created in the 1950s. It meant an increased role for the public sector and the building of a welfare society. This led, amongst other things, to a breakthrough for women in the labour market as they became employees in the public sector in healthcare and social services and education.[7] The changes meant that the management model MBI did not meet the new need to quickly react to change and managers needed to be able to make strategic decisions to a greater extent to be able to control but also encourage their employees. The goal of managing for production was replaced and was now about improving results, Management by Objectives (MBO), target setting, became the new management model.

MBO is still the management model that constitutes how we manage companies, organisations and the public sector today. The term was first used and defined by Peter Drucker (1954) in his book: *The Practice of Management*. The management and leadership model aims to improve accomplishments through clearly defined goals that the leadership/ managers and employees agree upon together. According to the theory, through having a set of goals and an action plan, you can increase participation and engagement in the employees and create agreement throughout the whole organisation regarding the goals.[8] The question is whether this model still works in the society, labour market and technological development of today and of the future.

In 1980, Simon L. Dolan published a book with a simple model about how we can achieve wellness at work, *Stress Santé et Rendement au Travail*. The question he asked after this was whether it was possible to create a culture where people's well-being was not affected negatively, or at least only in a minor way, and at the same time allow them to contribute to the organisation's productivity. In this question was the foundation for Management by Values. Together with the physicist Salvador Garcia he began discussing "healthy organisations" versus "unhealthy organisations". They saw that unhealthy organisations were characterised by a lack of mutual values, that insecurity dominated, that people were not cooperative and that leading executives used threats and manipulation to reach their goals.[9] The discussion led to them wanting to create a new culture in organisations and they wrote a book in Spanish that later became a bestseller in McGraw-Hill's series about leadership.

What is MBV then? Basically, it is a dynamic concept, that has developed since it was published in book form in 1997. The model is based on four connected trends that affect organisations' levels of complexity and uncertainty.

FOUR TRENDS[10]—THE BASIS OF MBV

1. **The need for quality and customer orientation**. Today's tough competition requires continuous quality improvements be offered to the consumer; it is not enough to offer just a standardised product.
2. **The need for professional autonomy and responsibility**. New technology, from robotisation and process automation to digitalisation has increased the need for employees to be highly professional and highly skilled. It places expectations on the employer to offer some room for independence and for employees to be willing to take responsibility.
3. **The need for "bosses" to evolve into leaders and facilitators**. Leadership is much more complex than only giving orders and supervising. The complexity increases in unison with employees' greater expectation for independence, flexibility and responsibility.
4. **The need for "flatter" and more agile organisational structures**. The global economy places new requirements on organisational structures: to be able to act quickly to new conditions; to be a fluid organisation based on networks, project teams, different strategic entities; and leave the standardised models for decentralising. See Figure 3.1.

Simon L. Dolan believes that the most important skill for 21st-century leaders and managers to learn is how to put values into practice. MBV is both a philosophy and a guide to application for leaders and managers on how one places focus on the organisation's core values and how they are then in line with the jointly developed strategic targets. This doesn't mean

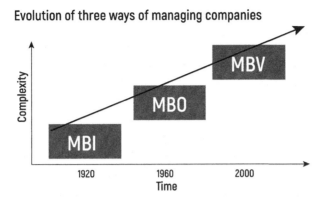

Evolution of three ways of managing companies

FIGURE 3.1

The evolution in the 20th century of three different ways to manage and lead organisations through instructions (MBI), goals (MBO) or values (MBV). Inspiration for the picture comes from *Managing by Values*. Dolan, S. L., Garcia, S. and Richley, B. (2006). *Managing by Values, A Corporate Guide to Living, Being Alive, and Making a Living in the 21st Century.* London: Palgrave, page 6. "Figure 1.1 Evolution of three ways of managing companies: by instructions, by objectives and by values". Note from the book: The conceptualisation is based on ideas put forward by Richard Norman in a seminar on organisational learning held in Stockholm in 1992. Figure created by Norlins förlag.

that values negate the need for goals or instructions. The values make both the goals and instructions understandable, meaningful and accepted. Figures 3.2 and 3.3 are two tables that, in short, show the differences between MBI, MBO and MBV.

Management by Values is based on a triaxial model for value management, of values-based leadership. It is used to identify the business/organisation's core values. From this, one can build a culture and formulate the organisation's strategic goals in line with core values and to understand the model is central to being able to use MBV. An organisation's values system which directly impacts how we behave consists of three dimensions as illustrated by the triaxial 3E-model.[11] Below is one possible categorisation of values which can be used to see which values are the organisation's core values.

A. **Economic-pragmatic values**: These values are about being efficient, high performance expectations and discipline. They are needed to guide activities around planning, quality control and accounting. These values are important for maintaining and assembling different subsystems in the organisation.

Differences from a strategic perspective between the management models
MBI, MBO and MBV

Characteristics	MBI	MBO	MBV
Reach of strategic vision	Short term	Medium term	Long term
Need for tolerance of ambiguity	Low	Medium	High
Philosophy of control	Top-down control, supervision	Control and stimulation of professional performace	Self-supervision encouraged
Organizational purpose	Maintain production	Optimize results	Continually improve processes

FIGURE 3.2

The table shows some differences between the management models MBI, MBO and MBV from a strategic perspective. For example, we see that MBV is about long-term and continual improvements. Inspiration for the picture comes from *Managing by Values* and Professor Natalia Guseva. Dolan, S. L., Garcia, S. and Richley, B. (2006). *Managing by Values, A Corporate Guide to Living, Being Alive, and Making a Living in the 21st Century.* London: Palgrave Macmillan, Page 15. Guseva, N. Management by instructions versus management by values in Russia: Pros and cons. https://www.hse.ru/data/2013/08/31/1270372062/Guseva%20Natalia%20%2011%20Internat%20Conference.pdf (07 June 2017).

B. **Ethical-social values**: These values are based on our beliefs, understanding, about how people should behave publicly, at work and in relationships. Social values such as honesty, congruity, respect and loyalty are closely connected to ethical values. A person's ethical values affect how the person behaves and performs when the other two values types in the model are used. In short, these values mirror how a person behaves when with others.

C. **Emotional-developmental values**: These values are closely connected to trust, freedom and happiness. Examples of these values are creativity/ideas, life/self fulfilment, assertiveness/managing and adaptability/flexibility. These are the basis for creating new opportunities for action. See Figures 3.4 and 3.5.

The triaxial model shows that each organisation's core consists of values that are built on three different dimensions: ethical, economic and emotional. The organisation's culture then shows to what extent the different values are enforced. MBV is about merging these three dimensions with strategic goals.

Differences from a tactical and operative perspective between the
management models MBI, MBO and MBV

Characteristics	MBI	MBO	MBV
Type of organizational structure	Multi-tiered pyramid	Pyramids with few levels	Networks, functional alliances, project teams
Need for autonomy, responsibility	Low	Medium	High
Leadership type	Traditional	Focused on resource allocation	Transformational (Legitimizes transformations)
Average level of professionalism of organization´s members	Management of operatives	Management of employees	Management of professionals
Core cultural values	Quantitative production. Loyalty, Conformity, discipline	Measuring results. Rationalization motivation, efficiency	Developing participation, continuous learning. Creativity mutual trust, commitment

FIGURE 3.3

The table shows some differences between the management models MBI, MBO and
MBV from a tactical and operative perspective. Inspiration for the picture was taken
from *Managing by Values* and Professor Natalia Guseva. Dolan, S. L., Garcia, S. and
Richley, B. (2006). Managing by Values, A Corporate Guide to Living, Being Alive, and
Making a Living in the 21st Century. London: Palgrave Macmillan, Page 15. Guseva, N.
Management by instructions versus management by values in Russia: Pros and cons.
https://www.hse.ru/data/2013/08/31/1270372062/Guseva%20Natalia%20%2011%20
Internat%20Conference.pdf (07 June 2017).

Values have previously been seen as "soft skills" and not so concrete
and solid. Values are therefore sometimes considered to not be important
enough to be a part of management and leadership, but more and more are
realising that they are the core of organisational strategy. The 3E-model is
a tool to find, bring forward or formulate an organisation's core values. The
leaders of today and of the future must be able to identify organisations'
values systems, according to what Simon Dolan says.[12] Leaders must be
able to communicate, internally and externally, the key position that the
values have. Then the organisation can succeed in reaching jointly set
goals. One must be able to match the organisation's structure and business
processes with its own value system. What this does is creates a framework

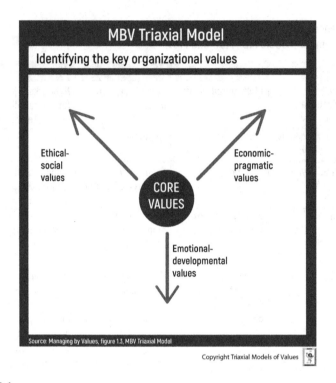

FIGURE 3.4
The three dimensions in the triaxial 3E-model for the management model MBV. Used with permission from Simon L. Dolan. Figure created by Norlins förlag.

that ensures a greater compatibility between what is said and what is actually done. It takes away the gap between the strategic intentions and the daily activities for everyone within the organisation, from the most senior boss to the newly employed. For sustainable leadership, one needs the underlying values behind every decision and activity to be clear and understandable for everyone in the organisation.

MBV aims to reduce the negative effects that come with the growing complexity that companies and organisations have ahead of them. An organisation that has clear, accepted and mutual values will be more effective at accommodating creativity and benefitting from the complexity and uncertainty. It will have major competitive advantages over organisations that only work from specific goals, and even more over those that only follow guidelines and documents.

Simon L. Dolan is responsible today for Future of Work at the ESADE university in Barcelona. He lectures around the world and continues to develop tools to support a values-based leadership. He is and has been a

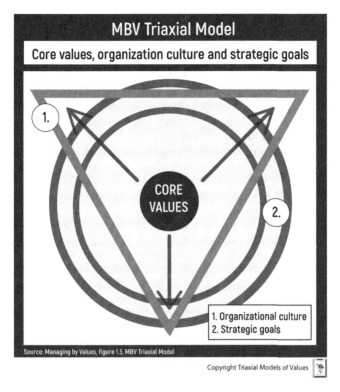

FIGURE 3.5
The relationship between an organisation's core values, organisational culture and strategic goals through the triaxial 3E-model. Used with permission from Simon L. Dolan. Figure created by Norlins förlag.

valuable sounding board in the writing of this book and a true inspiration during more difficult periods in my work.

It is of course my analysis and understanding of MBV that is presented in this book. It isn't a magic wand that I want to deliver but I want to introduce a reasoning and open a dialogue. I am convinced that we have a lot to do to develop our leadership in a time where complexity is increasing and where challenges and opportunities are in constant and quick change.

NOTES

1. Dolan, S. L., Garcia, S. and Richley B. (2006). *Managing by Values, A Corporate Guide to Living, Being Alive and Making a Living in the 21st Century.* London: Palgrave Macmillan, page 9.

2. Dolan, S. L., Garcia, S. and Richley, B. (2006). *Managing by Values, A Corporate Guide to Living, Being Alive, and Making a Living in the 21st Century*. London: Palgrave Macmillan.

3. Dolan, S. L., Garcia, S. and Richley, B. (2006). *Managing by Values, A Corporate Guide to Living, Being Alive, and Making a Living in the 21st Century*. London: Palgrave Macmillan, page 207.

4. Hedberg, K. and Melin, A. (2004). Vad ligger bakom "knäet" på industrisysselsättningskurvan? Linköping Universitet. http://liu.diva-portal.org/smash/get/div a2:19520/FULLTEXT01.pdf (07 June 2017).

5. Guseva, N. (2011). Management by instructions versus management by values in Russia: Pros and cons. https://www.hse.ru/data/2013/08/31/1270372062/Guse va%20Natalia%20%2011%20Internat%20Conference.pdf (07 June2017).

6. Schön, L. (2000). *En modern svensk ekonomisk historia—Tillväxt och omvandling under två sekel*. Stockholm: SNS Förlag.

7. Schön, L. (2000). *En modern svensk ekonomisk historia—Tillväxt och omvandling under två sekel*. Stockholm: SNS Förlag.

8. Hayes, A. (2017). Investopedia. Management by Objectives—MBO. http://www .investopedia.com/terms/m/management-by-objectives.asp (07 June 2017).

9. Dolan, S. L., Garcia, S. and Richley, B. (2006). *Managing by Values, A Corporate Guide to Living, Being Alive, and Making a Living in the 21st Century*. London: Palgrave Macmillan, Pages 208–209.

10. Ibid., pages 7–12.

11. Dolan, S. L., Garcia, S. and Richley, B. (2006). *Managing by Values, A Corporate Guide to Living, Being Alive, and Making a Living in the 21st Century*. London: Palgrave Macmillan, Page 14.

12. Dolan, S. L., Garcia, S. and Richley, B. (2006). *Managing by Values, A Corporate Guide to Living, Being Alive, and Making a Living in the 21st Century*. London: Palgrave Macmillan, Page 25.

4

What Are Those Values?

Values are the ideals that have the greatest importance in our lives. They are the rules we have chosen to control our priorities and actions, and they permeate all we do. Our values are nothing we have received or something that has happened—we have carefully chosen them in an internal process that at the same time excluded other values, and we are proud of them.

Valuesonline[1]

At Pascal's place, the school's first Team Lead met Petra Håkansson, Pieter Strijdom and Jens Hall before the school started for the first time. They sat together and looked at what Internationella Engelska Skolan stands for, they discussed what it meant to feel safe, what was meant by having an international perspective, and to see and cater to each and every student as an individual.

"We put a lot of time into analysing what IES stands for and how we wanted IESS (the school in Sundsvall) to incorporate and express this".

Pascal states that they dissected the ethics and the approach of Internationella Engelska Skolan (IES) as a company and as an organisation. The next step was to carefully think about and discuss how this would be relevant to a successful school in Sundsvall. When the discussions were done, they wrote a text together that described everything the school would stand for: "What We Stand For".

"The text gave us a clear direction".

During the interviews with Pascal, we have often ended up in a conversation about what values are, what differentiates them from things you believe in, culture or ethics? Or are they the same thing? This chapter is about how we should understand values and culture and ethics and what differentiates them from each other.. What importance do values have for Engelska Skolan Sundsvall and the leadership there and for all kinds of organisations? To be able to make full use of a value-based leadership, one must have an understanding of the terms and how they are connected. Furthermore, it helps to understand the reasons for the success both within the IES in general but also more clearly in Sundsvall.

There are three terms in psychology and literature that are closely related to the concept of values: beliefs, norms and attitudes. Simon L. Dolan believes that it is important that they are understood both independently but also in relation to each other and in which order they are built and developed:

> I have said that values can generally be understood as the strategic choices we make regarding what is required to achieve our goals. It is important to recognize that these choices, in turn, are derived from basic suppositions or beliefs about human nature and the world around us.[2]

In order to define the terms, I'm taking the advice of a true guru in this area, that the simple and perhaps most basic and obvious can still easily be abstract and difficult to define. However, the boundaries between the terms can be discussed, as well as what concerns your organisation, or for that matter, you as a person. The meaning crystallises through dialogue and after a lot of thought. Simon L. Dolan problematises and solidifies a lot around the concepts in his literature and has both studied and dedicated himself to the subject. It therefore feels natural to use his conclusions to explain the concepts in this book. If you want more information, read his books *Managing by Values*[3] and *Coaching by Values*.[4] See Figure 4.1.

─────

BELIEFS

Our convictions are very deeply grounded in thought patterns that we develop through years of learning and experiences; these thought patterns help us to explain and understand our reality. It is these thought patterns that in turn help to form our values. There is a subtle difference between convictions and values because of how closely related they are. This explains my quite long conversation with Pascal about whether Internationella

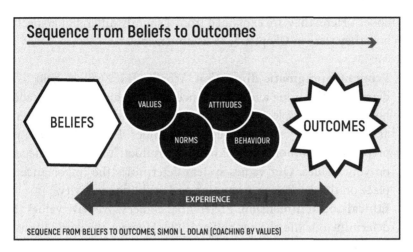

FIGURE 4.1
A picture of how beliefs are connected to an organisation's outcome, and a description of the position of values in the chain. The picture comes from the book *Coaching by Values*. Dolan, S. L. (2011). *Coaching by Values*. iUniverse, Page 87. Used with permission from Simon L. Dolan. Figure created by Norlins förlag.

Engelska Skolan's "What We Stand For! What We Believe In" is just about values or something else. An important difference is that our convictions, that is, what we believe in, come before the creation of values. If one wants to change values, one must also change convictions.

VALUES

Values are formed in childhood and youth based on what we have gotten from parents, teachers, friends and others. We learn values, often unconsciously, and we transfer them. Others' values that we come across in life affect us and our own values affect others. One can define values in many different ways; here is one of Dolan's definitions "the ideals that give significance to our lives, that are reflected in the priorities that we choose, and that we act on consistently and repeatedly".[5] From the perspective that values are ideals, values are therefore both tools and objectives for social transformation and to change society.

The foundation for Management by Values (MBV) is to see values from three perspectives and categorise them from these, the so called

"3E-model". Here, they are explained from a slightly different perspective than how they were in Chapter 3, 3E as dimensions:[6]

1. **Economic-pragmatic dimension**: Worth. These values help us to determine the value and importance of something. It can be about how we judge people, things, ideas, behaviour, feelings and facts. You assess a product's value through your values. For example, are you prepared to pay more for an ecological product? Yes, that can depend on your values. Our values system determines the importance we place on the workplace promoting and enabling creativity.

2. **Ethical-social dimension**: Preferential choices. We have values that determine our life choices and attitude. How we see work, lifestyle, family life and so on. Are we driven by success or distress? How dependent we are on other people or our job is based on values about independence. These values are shown in how we act rather than in the words we say.

3. **Emotional-developmental dimension**: Personal fulfilment. What makes each individual happy and what one feels a sense of satisfaction about varies from person to person and even from culture to culture. These values are related to happiness and freedom. They are the motivation that drives people to achieve their dreams. There is much indication that these values have the greatest influence on our behaviour. Dolan sees that feeling secure in these values has a bearing on whether a person is able to reach their full potential. See Figure 4.2.

Simon L. Dolan
Coaching by Values

"When one is confident about his or her emotional-developmental values, dreams that once seemed too risky and too far beyond one's capabilities now appear not only reasonable but compelling. This security allows one to live up to one's potential and accomplish dreams that in early stages of one's life may have been too frightening to embrace."

FIGURE 4.2

Coaching by Values. Dolan, S. L. (2011). *Coaching by Values*. iUniverse, Page 84.

NORMS

Values in turn have a particular role in building norms, norms which Dolan calls "rules of the game".[7] Values are nothing constant but are generated and strengthened through an individual's life. Norms, on the other hand, are created and appear through interaction with others. They are our rules of conduct, codes of conduct, adopted by consensus. Our values cause us to evaluate, accept or reject norms. The differences between these two concepts also become clear from what happens when we go against them. When we go against norms, there are external sanctions, in the form of strong reactions from others, but it can also be punishment such as fines or jail time. When we go against values, there's more of an "internal" sanction, the result being guilt and/or shame.

ATTITUDES

Many times, I have heard myself say: "You have to change your attitude" or "Your attitude determines how you experience everything you meet and where you find yourself". Especially when working with teenagers in the school environment. Of course, one's attitude affects how people perceive you and even what you manage to achieve in your day-to-day work. The classic analogy of what determines if you are a person with a positive attitude or not is if you see the glass as half full or half empty. But I have never really thought about how we could change or affect our attitude deep down before. Is it just a "mindset", is that all that's needed? In the school world, the attitude between teachers and students and vice versa is important from many perspectives. I am also thinking of something that has received a greater focus in the public sector in recent years, a good customer relationship. The attitude I find from the person who answers the phone; that determines my experience. The word attitude is used routinely and Dolan sees that the confusion around the concept in that researchers in the areas of management, organisational development and psychology feel that it is easier to measure attitudes instead of values.[8] He defines attitudes as being a consequence of those values and norms that precede the attitudes. Our attitudes reflect how we feel for someone or something and predict how we will probably act in a given situation.

BEHAVIOUR AND OUTCOMES

If attitude is a feeling, an opinion, or approval/ like or dislike for something, then behaviour is the way we act and react. Our behaviours are more often than not a reflection of our convictions, values and attitudes. But our behaviour is also affected by other factors such as our predetermined perceptions about ourselves and others, economic factors, social impact and norms; behaviour can even be affected by what fits best and feels simplest there and then.

HOW IT COMES TOGETHER

In a business or in an organisation, big or small, it is important to understand the connection and reasons to be able to make those changes needed and to communicate what is important at the company. To manage by values is to formulate and work with what will later affect norms, attitudes, behaviour and in the end, the conduct and result. Dolan has a picture to depict the connection (Figure 4.1). It is interesting to use this picture to help understand oneself. To try to put yourself in the model is a good way to understand the subtleties between the concepts. This is a tool for analysing an existing organisation but also when you start something new. The way beliefs, values, norms, attitudes, behaviours and outcomes interact is a process in constant motion and is therefore not something one simply decides at one point in time and then puts aside. Daily awareness and active work are necessary at the individual level, in a company or for an entire community. Together the different parts promote something very tangible, namely organisational and company culture, which I will discuss further in the next chapter.

VALUES MORE CONCRETE

On Internationella Engelska Skolan's website under the title: *Ethical Guidelines,*[9] it says that the school has been driven by strong values since its beginning in 1993. They formulate there what they call their "core beliefs", that is their fundamental beliefs:

1. The need for a calm and orderly learning environment, in which teachers can teach and students learn.
2. The importance of learning to command the English language, as the key to the world.
3. The value of showing high expectations for every student, irrespective of their background, and preaching the norm of working hard, through thick and thin, to reach your full potential.

Then they write that Internationella Engelska Skolan promises as an organisation to always put these beliefs at the centre of everything. Leaders on all levels have the task of working for them first and foremost. Their organisation discloses them as strong in norms and values. No matter who I spoke with in the school's organisation, from CEO to different people on staff, the subject school's founder, Barbara Bergström always came up. What she personifies and wanted to create over 25 years ago still characterises the whole organisation. Even if practical adjustments are done at the different schools concerned, the foundation she laid plays a decisive role in the business and is what drives development.

What Barbara and IES do and have done is something one can see not just in their work with values, but also in their work with beliefs, which they started one step earlier. These beliefs have different terms and concepts, but in the end, the concepts are not central, the important thing is the clarity that takes shape in everything done in what is today a large business concern. It was here that Pascal began his work when the school was to establish itself in Sundsvall, when he and his first colleagues analysed the school's convictions in depth in order to understand what it would mean in Sundsvall. This year he has put in extra effort into something he calls "back to basics". Now with the school continuing to grow at the same time as having many on staff having worked there for many years, proper work is needed to remind them of the most fundamental points: What we believe in and how that affects everything we do at school. Vice principal, Petra Håkansson, believes that in his role as principal, Pascal never moves away from the values. Nothing that is said at the school's assemblies is said by chance and the focus is on what they believe in. In the systematic quality work, the school has had different themes through the years, but these themes have always been connected to that school's beliefs and mutual values. We would never work with something that isn't linked to our three pillars. Our work environment is very important, we paint basically every summer. When we got mild criticism on the environment in the toilets, it became a management focus straight away. We have English as the working language at school, to speak English is a natural part of their everyday for our students. So every student can reach their full potential, we have as a starting point: "No child left behind" and "Tough love".

She believes that the school has a good basic structure so everything would continue to work well no matter what the leadership might be and in Pascal's absence for a time. But for that to last in the long run, she sees him as extremely important—if he didn't lead by good example, why would others follow what was decided? The entire leadership team must follow rules and behaviour and need to be constantly present in the organisation.

> We all must pick up that piece of rubbish lying on the floor, otherwise the system falls. And it is of great importance that for example Pascal himself participates in the school's fun run, he is very present in the school's activities.

It isn't enough to formulate a number of well-chosen values for them to characterise an organisation and be a key to success. It is obvious in Pascal's leadership that it is daily strategic work that also shows itself in how he behaves himself. Obviously, in Pascal's leadership there is the daily strategic work but also how he himself behaves in the organisation. What, therefore, is central in the formation of values in an organisation? In the book *Coaching by Values*,[10] there are some things that are considered to be of particular importance.

1. **The beginning** of a company or organisation is central. The founder's values and beliefs have an impact on whether the company will grow or not. Organisations that have a strong cultural identity often succeed in upholding the strength that the founder stood for. Here I see very clearly how this is true for Internationella Engelska Skolan where the founder Barbara Bergström is still an important person, almost mythological. Her values are valued as the most important for the leadership concerned and likewise for the staff in each school.

2. **The beliefs and values** in the present leadership as well as the system in place for what is rewarded in the organisation. At any time, it is possible for the organisation's management to modify or change the values the founder stands/stood for. There is always a balance between preserving and renewing, to be traditional or to modernise. This balance is often central to whether a company will be successful for generations. The present management's view of values, old and new, of course shape the organisation. In my interviews with Pascal and people on the leadership team in Sundsvall, it is clear that they have chosen to continue to work for the values that guided them from the beginning. But that doesn't mean a leadership that just leans back, they work every day to implement the values and think about how they are relevant today and in the future. For management's beliefs and values to be the same for other employees, there must be mechanisms in place that encourage different behaviours in the organisation. An example of this could be that if one has the value of a calm study environment in the classroom, then it isn't enough to hold lovely speeches about it; management must engage and make a calm study environment possible. Management needs to acknowledge and stimulate a calm study environment and encourage it. Pascal often returns to the idea that his and management's job is to make it possible for teachers to be teachers and this is done for example through giving extra resources and support; clear rules; and a principal that often visits the classroom.

3. **Education and training**. There is a need for continuous education and training on the values one wants to characterise the organisation with and also to untrain those values that one doesn't want to have in the organisation. New staff or staff that have worked for a long time in an organisation often need to "unlearn" and forget what one has previously learnt, according to Dolan. It isn't enough to just focus on those values one wants to work with but one must also analyse and work on avoiding those values one doesn't want. One can go through courses and conferences and read books, but often one needs to work more actively than that; there needs to be coaches. According to Dolan, to coach is: "the art of bringing out the greatness in people in a way that honors the person's integrity of the human spirit. It is both an innate human capacity and a teachable skill".[11] Briefly described, according to Dolan the following characteristics are

necessary for every professional coach: knowledge about coaching; knowledge about relationships; the ability to listen; the ability to be autonomous; the ability to investigate and ask questions; the ability to provide feedback; the ability to work on goals, values and beliefs; and finally the ability to bring forward concrete actions and tasks for the person one is coaching.[12]

Middle management is a function where the coaching qualities become important for secure continuity over time. When Pascal talks about his leadership team, I realise that he has chosen very carefully which people are a part of the team. They are there because they complement each other, because they are people who fit as leaders and everyone in the leadership team stands completely behind the school's beliefs and way of working. In what can be perceived as a controlled and managed organisation, one might expect that the people who work there never question and that the leadership team is made up of nothing but Yes men. Perhaps it is here that makes them later become good coaches in the organisation, they are clear and follow up what has been decided, but they have a deep understanding for why one should do something. Even if the word coach never came up in interviews, I see Internationella Engelska Skolan Sundsvall as having working methods centred around coaching. The leaders that work there want to support all staff in being able to deliver what the school has promised students and parents. When it then comes to professional development in education, a lot of time is put into the school's three beliefs and one substantiates what it means in values and actions.

"It is easy to believe that there isn't time to discuss and work with the soft values, but we have chosen to take time for it, we need to know who we are and what we will deliver". It is the leader's responsibility to see that it is prioritised, says Pascal.

4. **Laws.** A country's laws affect beliefs and values both in companies and organisations. They affect how we see the work environment and working conditions for our employees. Sweden's anti-discrimination laws have an effect on our Swedish companies and affect corporate culture. The tax system and fees govern even those values and in turn behaviour. Internationella Engelska Skolan chooses when describing their "Ethical Guidelines" to even include legislation as something

that should be followed but also something they want to engage in and influence for the better.

5. **Your branch's specific conditions**. Your organisation is influenced by the context in which it finds itself. Is it a competitive business or not? Do you see yourself as a competitor, rival or colleague in the branch? This can influence how one thinks in the short and long term. Here one can think about how the "game rules" in a specific branch influence values. The Swedish school system with both government and non-government schools influences even schools' values. In the discussions with Pascal, we have thought a lot about what challenges or possibilities there are in being a non-government school. If a school is to continue to exist, especially in an environment where competition exists, it needs to deliver and remain good. When the school in Sundsvall grows, one needs to continuously and over time convince more and more children and parents that this school is a good choice. In the competitive situation, the economic value can be that one needs a specific number of students. If we connect this to the 3E-model, this value is important for the organisation's survival.

6. **The current social values**. Each time and each society have their specific social values. This of course affects leaders and entrepreneurs but it also affects the employee attitude and approach. How well a company is in sync with current social values affects the possibility of attracting employees. When the company's values are in sync with the society's social values, there will also be less social clashes. It makes a work environment possible where you feel comfortable. An example of this can be openness and fairness. Internally in the organisation, it has a lot to do with communication. Do the employees get the information before they see it in the paper? How much transparency do you get from the company? Externally, it can be about transparency and the availability of information. An example from Internationella Engelska Skolan Sundsvall (IESS) where they realise that openness is important is around grades. They are very open with how they work with grade setting. Internally, it is something they discuss a lot and analyse together.

"The correlation between the national test results and the students' grade is important for us and is therefore something we work hard with", says Pascal.

In communication with parents and students, they use amongst other things an intranet. On the intranet, teachers communicate continuously about comments and grades about how students perform against the course plan. If the school does not manage the grading issue in a responsible and professional way, the image of the organisation would probably change. If an organisation breaks the current social values, it becomes negative for the organisation's attractiveness and competitive power.

7. **The society's tradition and culture**. A society's history affects the business culture and expectations. Different countries have different motivations. What is it that drives Sweden's business culture? We feel proud of our internationally recognised brands, our raw materials such as our forests and ore, a strong commodity and manufacturing industry, music industry and we see our IT sector as an opportunity to continue to be a successful nation. In the political debate, one often hears the argument that companies are crucial for securing welfare. Is it this which is the motivation behind new companies? Is the motivation to get smaller companies to grow and our larger companies to continue to have their base in Sweden? I don't know the answer, but the question is interesting and the answer influences which values are formed in our company. Is the value to do good for the society or is it that we must improve to not allow Asia all too large a piece of the global market pie? School has its story. Today school should be neutral except for some basic values formulated in the school law. It wasn't like this if we were to go back to my parents' generation, where hymns and morning prayer were part of the day-to-day. My father talks about his organ test before he became a qualified teacher—you had to be able to play the organ in the classroom as part of your teacher qualification—it was not that long ago. Sweden has a strong tradition that school must be free because of our society's aspiration that everyone should have the same opportunities. That government schools exist at all is still discussed. Today's great challenge seems to be to find a system to provide equivalent schools for all students in Sweden. As a leader in a school, you need to be familiar with all these discussions and values about school in your strategic work. In working with values in an organisation, you need to know which social values

characterise the society that the company is in and have knowledge about the society where you run your organisation. It is interesting to think about how Internationella Engelska Skolan Sundsvall has been able to become so popular in a municipality where there is a lot of resistance to non-government schools and a municipal council where academy traditionally hasn't been especially strong. It is perhaps not the society that one would have expected a school with this profile to have had such a strong impact on. But somehow, IESS has succeeded in meeting all the social values that characterise Sundsvall as a city; otherwise they would not have been able to grow as they have.

8. **The company's prosperity or shortcomings**. As long as a company goes well, one doesn't usually question the values. Prosperity is often something that keeps the values alive. But if it starts to go badly for a company, perhaps there is a great failure, it's then that one probably starts to assess one's values. It can be quite a difficult journey. Are the values wrong or have you perhaps not worked with them enough? Internationella Engelska Skolan in Sweden is growing in number of schools and students, and can be seen as a prosperous company that runs a good school organisation. Should they not deliver a good school organisation, the company would not grow. All organisations go through failures and parts of the organisation that don't go well; in this specific company, they have chosen to keep to their values. In the discussions with Pascal, there is a fear that the school will one day fail its task, he works hard and consciously for that not to happen, the fear is a part of what drives him. If that happened, it would be interesting to see if one would then begin to think about if the values needed to be changed, that they have gotten out of date or perhaps simply are wrong, or if the reason for the failure should be searched for in other areas.

Values do not exist in a vacuum and their creation and survival are complex. Not all values are good either; some can be damaging for an organisation, for you as a person or for a society. Managing by values isn't about being good, to have "the right values", but it is about a way to manage and lead. Values are so central because they have such a strong impact on the final result, what we actually do and accomplish. Values also have the ability to unite and create context, which in turn can be made to create something good or to destroy. The conclusion nevertheless is that having knowledge about values is advantageous both for an organisation's development but also in being in competition with others.

When you start to map values, if they are your own or an organisation's, you might realise that there is a lot to them. Here the previously named triaxial 3E-model is a tool for sorting; you must also realise that our values are in a strong hierarchy in relation to each other. When you in the end make a choice, it isn't certain that all your values will point in the same direction, and then you must make a choice using the hierarchy. When Internationella Engelska Skolan Sundsvall stands before a problem, a challenge, they must choose which of the three values they will turn to and against. One must know which is highest in the hierarchy. This will facilitate when decisions must be made and when one needs to find a consensus on an issue.

"We discuss a lot at the school, we can have big discussions but we know what we want to achieve the whole time. We also have a culture where once a decision has been made, everyone stands behind it", says Pascal.

Finally, in this chapter, we also need to ask ourselves if values can be measured in some way? We Swedes love to be able to measure things. The perception that values are difficult to measure makes it easy for them to get an inconspicuous role when it is time for evaluations and to measure success. Of course, the more subjective the values are, the more difficult they are to measure quantitatively. A survey of employees can give answers for if one thinks the workplace promotes creativity for example, and then one can get statistics and set percentages as goals. The best way to measure is actually in an honest conversation with the relevant people at regular intervals. Here I return to one of Pascal's mantras:

> You must take time to talk about the softer values. You must do this without knowing exactly what it is you are achieving. What I know is that if you skip these conversations and discussions, it will cost you more in the end.

There is a lot more to say about values, it is a discussion that will continue. I hope that this chapter has given you a basic understanding to progress from in this discussion. In the next chapters, values will be a starting point for several different areas that challenge and enable leadership.

NOTES

1. Valuesonline. https://volwp.azurewebsites.net/?page_id=7&lang=sv (20 June 2017). Translation to English Marjorie Challis. (New website 2019 www.values.se.)
2. Dolan, S. L. (2011). *Coaching by Values*. iUniverse, Page 86.
3. Dolan, S. L., Garcia, S. and Richley, B. (2006). *Managing by Values, A Corporate Guide to Living, Being Alive, and Making a Living in the 21st Century*. London: Palgrave Macmillan.
4. Dolan, S. L. (2011). *Coaching by Values*. iUniverse.
5. Dolan, S. L. (2011). *Coaching by Values*. iUniverse, Page 93.
6. Dolan, S. L., Garcia, S. and Richley, B. (2006). *Managing by Values, A Corporate Guide to Living, Being Alive, and Making a Living in the 21st Century*. London: Palgrave Macmillan, Page 28–34.
7. Dolan, S. L., Garcia, S. and Richley, B. (2006). *Managing by Values, A Corporate Guide to Living, Being Alive, and Making a Living in the 21st Century*. London: Palgrave Macmillan, Page 37.
8. Dolan, S. L. (2011). *Coaching by Values*. iUniverse, Page 88.
9. Internationella Engelska Skolan. Ethical guidelines. https://engelska.se/sv/about-ies/ethical-guidelines (30 June 2017).
10. Dolan, S. L. (2011). *Coaching by Values*. iUniverse, Page 97–98.
11. Ibid., p. 8.
12. Ibid., pp. 13–14.

5

Culture Is No Copycat

Your organization's culture is the product of the people in it, and every addition and subtraction will alter the chemistry. Do everything you can to keep it harmonious.

Lee Cockerell[1]

When I go in through the quite heavy doors to Internationella Engelska Skolan Sundsvall (IESS), I immediately feel a certain atmosphere. Quite often, there are changes in the foyer, either something to do with the season, holidays or in connection with different school themes. Always stylish, clean and neat. The staff at reception greet me in a friendly manner and check that I know where I am going, and through this check that I am a person who should be visiting the school. It hits me every time, and there have been some times in recent months, where when I sit on the benches outside Pascal's office and wait for an interview that I am met with smiles. All the staff who pass look for eye contact and greet me happily. In the beginning, I remember that I was surprised and reacted to it, especially because my visits were late in the afternoons to not "disturb" Pascal during the hours that the school organisation is most intensive. I now want to introduce another concept that we have discussed a lot in our conversation, that is, culture. How is culture made? What is an organisation's culture? One can sort of "feel" the culture at Internationella Engelska Skolan Sundsvall. Many of the staff who I have interviewed say that their first contact with the school made them feel something. It really sits in the walls and is something very noticeable—at the same time it is difficult to touch. "When one comes into the building, there's an atmosphere, how one wants to be met, it's hard to describe. You want to be a part of it. The mutual goals are clearly formulated, we know what we believe in!" says Anna-Maria Allanius, assistant principal, on what made her want to work at the school in 2011.

Simon L. Dolan describes organisation culture as the organisation's personality. The culture consists of assumptions, values, norms and tangible symbols and signals that in the first place comes from the organisation's leadership and their behaviour. This is what Petra Håkansson, assistant principal thought on her first impression of Pascal, and how he was affected by mentors he got from IES:

> My first impression of Pascal, when we spoke the first time, was that he was so unbelievably correct. This was my first worry when leaving my employment at Internationella Engelska Skolan Järfälla and moving to Sundsvall to work at the new school there. Pascal expected us to be proper, and say, "yes ma'am" and "yes sir", and here I come in jeans and tattoos.

"So, you felt it was strict even though you came from another school in the same organisation?"

> Yes, there are differences. The clash became especially clear on one of Pascal's initiatives to advertise the school. We were to stand at IN Galleri (a shopping mall) in Sundsvall. I wore my T-shirt that had Internationella Engelska Skolan's logo over the whole stomach, and jeans. I thought they were the right clothes for the event. He came in a crisp suit, extremely correct. When it was time to stand at Birsta City (a different shopping mall), then I also had a more strict dress code. We are probably one of the best dressed schools in Sweden

says Petra, and laughs.

"How is it that Pascal is so particular about clothes—and manners do you think?"

> Partly it had to do with which mentors he had higher up in the organisation, he was a copy of them. Then it's Pascal as a person, regardless of the situation he finds himself in, he goes 'All in' and he is clear with what is expected of the rest of us.

From my own experience, I have seen how difficult it can be to get teachers or staff to stand behind different rules and behaviours, so I am impressed with how staff at the school follow the dress code, for example, why doesn't anyone make a fuss about the "no jeans rule"? Pascal takes up the dress code himself when we talk about culture and values.

"We have a strong culture of: 'We walk together' which in principle means that almost no one questions that we, for example, don't wear jeans to work". What then is the culture at Internationella Engelska Skolan Sundsvall and what is its importance? Pascal feels that they have a particular challenge to keep staff together, partly because they have grown quickly but first and foremost because they recruit many of their staff from Canada and other countries. The number of staff has grown every year and at the same time as the group grows, so does the cultural diversity. This he believes requires one to focus on that what is most mundane and basic. Here, the culture becomes important for shaping the team and creating a team that works together.

> A group of values that one puts together becomes a culture. We must continue to talk about our values, otherwise we lose our culture. When we get new staff, we put a lot of focus on what we believe, our convictions, how one should behave, and explain what it is that defines us. Part of our culture is, for example, that we are quick to answer emails. We also decide together what we will stand behind. One can't expect that everyone will just follow the culture, but if the culture is strong, most will follow.

"How do you motivate your employees to stand behind all your beliefs and how they should behave?"

> We explain why it is important and how every little bit is important for the whole. Then I need to as a leader realise that each person is an individual, who ultimately want to protect their own and survive. When it gets difficult to survive, values, which can be viewed as abstract, I usually explain for example how different behaviours can affect you as an individual and what happens if you don't do as we mutually decided. Everyone needs to understand the consequences, and how things are connected.

A close colleague of Pascal who has been there from the start, Pieter Strijdom, feels that it is much of Pascal's drive as well as fear and paranoia that has created a strong culture at the school, a culture that is built on clear values.

It is the paranoia that we will lose our culture and our beliefs that drives him to create, to challenge and drive us forward the whole time. It has meant that we have held together and become a community. It is because we carry our beliefs from year to year that we succeed and the focus from all staff is that we will preserve our culture. We all care for what we have and the fear of losing the great thing we have built, that motivates us to work with everything from values to behaviour.

"The cool thing is that we very rarely doubt that the people here will deliver", adds Pascal.

Another teacher feels that the strong culture has its foundation in the founder, Barbara Bergström. Amongst other things, her view that everyone is a "doer" or in other words, enabler and have the power to act. That one must continue to test and test, over and over again.

This is what we do in student care, it develops and changes the whole time, we test new ways so we can be as good as possible. If something doesn't work, then we go back to our values and from that, think about how we can do things differently

says Jens Hall.

When I converse with Pascal and his colleagues, they love to talk about the school's culture as a strong driving force and attraction. They describe it as a mixture of high expectations and a lot of jokes and laughter.

I was recruited in Canada when Pascal was there looking for staff. I have been here since the first year, I thought then that I would stay one or max two years. But the values and the school's culture, which is relaxed in that we joke a lot with each other, has made me stay. I think that a strong unity between us colleagues means that we have fun and that makes it possible for the school to grow quickly

says Jocelyn Beranger, head of houses and a teacher.

Pascal believes that the culture is a part of the school's success. But he also believes that the strong culture means that it is not a workplace for just anyone.

We have staff that have reacted and who react to our culture. That we encourage boldness and delivery on promises, means some feel stressed. It often becomes clear in job interviews if the person will fit in with us or not, both we leaders and the potential employee can feel it quite directly. Sometimes, one notices it with time. Of course, the school could be successful with another culture, but the culture we have has made the school what it is today

he says.

In this context, we will discuss Jeff Bezos and Amazon's company culture. A little detail on this context is that Pascal loves to read, especially literature written by or about strong leaders. References to books he has read have therefore often come up quite often in our discussions. He thinks that Amazon is a good example of a place where there is a strong company culture that permeates through the whole organisation from the founder to every employee. But just like for Internationella Engelska Skolan Sundsvall and for Amazon, it is a culture that fits there, you can't copy a culture as it is so much more complex than that.

Before we look closer at what characterises the culture at the school and how this affects the organisation, I want to go back to Internationella Engelska Skolan (IES) as a whole and their previously named "Ethical Guidelines for Internationella Engelska Skolan". On their website, you can read the guidelines and they have written The following about culture:

A culture of strong values in conviction and action cannot be regulated in every detail—that's why it is called a "culture". Every member of the IES organisation has a personal responsibility to act so that the culture is confirmed and renewed every day, with every action. Ask yourself:

- Is my way of acting and thinking in accordance with the core values of Internationella Engelska Skolan?
- Do I contribute to a positive, upbeat and constructive atmosphere in the school, and by my way of interacting with students and colleagues?
- Can I explain and defend my actions with a clear conscience, should they be scrutinized in public, for example in a newspaper article or through a school inspection?
- Do I contribute positively to the strong and good reputation of Internationella Engelska Skolan? This entails also how I am perceived outside of school, for example when a parent happens to run into me in a public environment. Impressions are created not only in school, but also by what others can see outside of school, including how I act on social media.

- What consequences could my behaviour have for IES and the school? Go for the good, dare to stand up for strong values. Try to be someone to emulate also in civil life.[2]

That the school in Sundsvall has a strong culture isn't a coincidence, it is a part of the concept. They work very consciously with the culture, discussing what affects it, and that everyone has a responsibility to create it. When I read the points, I see how they are clearly a part of Pascal's leadership, he himself always tries to have these perspectives close by for how he should act. These points explain many of the discussions we have had about this book, that his involvement has always needed to keep to the school's guidelines. I noticed in all the people I have interviewed that they are very possessive of the school. They are very open and there are many strong opinions in team lead but care for the school shines through in a strong way. Pieter Strijdom expresses it like this:

We see the school as if it were our own child, we care about it!

To give you a picture of the culture at Internationella Engelska Skolan Sundsvall, here are several descriptions from different people in the organisation. Teachers who have started, finished and come back; staff who have been there from the start; staff who haven't worked so long; and of course, we must look at a student's perspective too. I often meet people who have an image of the school in Sundsvall and that it is the discipline and strict rules that make the school successful. It is an all too simple view that does not reflect the whole behind what most who work in the organisation seem to be in agreement on—namely that it is "tough love" that makes the difference.

A present and active principal is something many have commented on when I have asked about Pascal's role at the school. He is in the classroom, out in the corridors, outside the school in the morning, in the lunch hall and at different activities making his way of being and his personality have a strong imprint on the whole organisation. "If it's the school fun run, Pascal is there and running! He sees everyone, is driven, wants us to grow and like activities", says Petra Håkansson, assistant principal.

"You can't hide at the school. You feel seen if you are five minutes late. This is both for students and staff", says Pieter Strijdom. The culture of constant presence in some way makes another strong characteristic of the school's culture possible—to act quickly.

Pieter continues: "We react quickly!"

This has also been confirmed by a previous student, Kim Åkerström, when he answers the question of how the school's values looked for him as a student:

> Almost the biggest thing about the school is how they manage different situations, for example, if there is a fight or bullying, normally something like that is difficult to sort out, but here, there is zero tolerance. The teachers and others at the school acted immediately and saw that they got to the bottom of the issue. All teachers were on the same page. They weren't afraid of conflicts and really acted.

Attention to detail and not leaving anything to chance is something that of course has something to do with the organisational culture of Internationella Engelska Skolan, but it is surely extra strong because of Pascal's constant drive to improve and anxiety about making mistakes. Mattias Nilsson, a teacher who moved to Sundsvall to work at the school but then left after five years and has now chosen to return to the school tells me: "Here, nothing is left to chance, and that comes from the founder Barbara: One doesn't leave anything to chance".

Karin Henriksson has been a part of the school since the beginning. At first, she worked half time in the kitchen and half time in reception and today she is a part of the team that works in administration. It is noticeable that she is one of the key people when it comes to making sure that things are developed and kept in order in all details.

> It is important how we welcome new teachers. Everyone should feel welcome and there is a little bit more to think about since many of our staff have moved to Sweden and Sundsvall and haven't been here before. Sometimes I even go to the doctor with them. We are very well organised and work hard so that all details will work, it is an important support for everyone who works here and, of course, for students and parents too. For us in administration, it is important to constantly improve and evolve. Just take the practical details around all the lockers and keys when we keep growing as a school. It needs to work smoothly. To constantly improve—that is a part of the culture at the school.

To continually improve, to evolve all the time, seems to be something that is crucial and because of which people will like being at the school or not. When one as a person feels that a workplace agrees with one's own values and one's own drive, one often enjoys working there. The opposite is also true; if one finds oneself in an environment that clashes too much with one's own beliefs, this can easily result in one not feeling comfortable and not feeling satisfaction. So, even from this perspective, a company's culture is important, it ultimately determines the employees who are there and who want to work there.

"If you don't like to develop yourself or to be a part of the development of an organisation, you usually don't want to work with us", says Jocelyn.

Pascal personifies in some way this part of the culture, as he himself described in the beginning of the book, he is driven to look for problems and fix everything. "We even sent messages to each other during a school show about how we could improve it for next year", says Pascal and smiles.

> When we in team lead went to Rhodes for training days, it was a tough pro-
> gramme that Pascal had planned in detail. He was so worried that someone
> would think that we took the school's money and went on holiday. It was
> quite a tough week

says Pieter and laughs.

Order and somewhat authoritarian culture are what many expect of Internationella Engelska Skolan. This is connected to their promise of a calm study environment and high expectations of students. It is very much about being clear, that everyone should know what is expected and what happens if one doesn't do what is expected. The rules are communicated early, clearly and regularly. Parents know what is expected before they say yes to their child's place at the school and as a parent, you are expected to go through the rules together with your child. Children and adolescents quickly learn that the wrong behaviour has consequences and most are aware that they are expected to follow the rules. When something is decided, then the staff are also expected to follow it and act in the way that was decided. If something is decided, there is no room for your own creativity. If you want to change something, you must take it up for discussion and not until a new decision has been made can you act differently.

"We go in the same direction, we have the same rules. Here we talk about 'we' and not 'I'", says Karin Henriksson.

"At our weekly meetings, it isn't just information but also our beliefs, 'What we believe in', that is always present in some way", says Pieter.

The weekly meeting makes things clear for staff what is happening during the week but also clarifies how they should work, from which focus. The clarity is on several levels.

Everyone who was there at the end of school for summer celebration in 2017 can see how hundreds of students walk in nice lines from the school to Tonhallen (a concert hall where they have their end of school year celebrations amongst other things) and that many prizes were given out for school achievements and there is a lot of joy, jokes and humour. The stage is decorated with big glitter numbers 2017, and pretty matching flowers. The programme commences solemnly with the national anthem. I suspect that the person who drew the most smiles was a performance where Pascal in sunglasses, dances together with a student named Olivia Fisher on the stage. As well as a fun show, it was clearly connected to something deeper. He explains that a few weeks earlier, he was walking around the corridors and in the lunch hall in the school. He photographed students and they had to answer the question: "What makes you you?", he asked from the stage if the students remember that. The dance on the stage was about Olivia's answer to that question—for her, dance was an important part of who she is. Pascal then gives all the students some homework over the summer; they must think about what makes them who they are. He also explains that this is a question that describes something that is a part of Internationella Engelska Skolan, to be able to feel safe and therefore to be yourself.

"If you know who you are, then we can also create a school where you can be who you are!" says Pascal from the stage.

Nothing is random, not even the fun part of the end of year celebrations. The programme continues, and then comes a short film from the teachers with a lot of humour and a glint in their eyes. In what is today a large elementary school, they make an effort to create warm relationships between teachers, staff and students. One sees this again in the school's different theme days where one dresses up and does different activities, to foster a community. Again, Pascal usually does his best and from what I understand, he has quite a large store of dress up clothes so he is ready for both "Haunted House" at Halloween or for a vegetable day at the school. See Figure 5.1.

This joy and warmth also create a culture of community. Here they say hello to each other, anything else is unthinkable. When their employees from different countries move to Sundsvall, one makes sure to take them to shopping centres and anywhere else they need to go, so they can have

FIGURE 5.1
Principal Pascal Brisson inspires students to eat more vegetables in the school's cafeteria.
Photo: Jody Thompson, Still Vision Photography.

a good start in a new country. Many of the staff say they become like a family. The school also has retirees as volunteers and this seems to have also contributed to a warmer atmosphere. This specific part of the culture strengthens the possibility for something Pascal often goes back to: At this workplace, we walk together.

> There is a consensus here amongst the staff. We have a lot of fun together. I was there from when the school started then left to work as a principal at another school. When I came back, I immediately felt the culture. Even if a lot had happened at the school, the culture was still the same

says Jens Hall, teacher at the school. See Figure 5.2.

During one of my interviews, I was able to see this in practice. In the middle of the interview, Pascal gets an SMS and he asks if it's OK if he

FIGURE 5.2
We walk together. Photo: Pascal Brisson.

steps out for a minute as there is something he must help solve before the next week. This was on Friday afternoon and the time was already 5pm. He is gone some minutes and then he comes back.

"We just found out that we won't be able to use the lunch hall next week because of the renovations", he says and sounds much calmer than I thought would be expected.

"Oh, perhaps you want to continue the interview another time so you can solve this?"

"No, it's no worries, there are several of us that will stay until it is solved. We decided to make something good out of it and create the feeling that it is a summer picnic in the corridors", he says and looks very satisfied.

Here I saw the strength in how they work together. They are used to quickly finding solutions and take opportunities to do something even better than planned despite standing before quite a big challenge.

Perhaps what I have just described could be another way and example of a culture that they themselves call "tough love". I still want to show the complexity of describing a culture. As always, it is important to define and describe words and concepts because they mean such different things for different people and in different situations. One of the school's previous students, Kim Åkerström, that I interviewed connected the concept to respect and trust. When I asked him to describe what defines the school, he said:

> The first thing I think of is the respect between students and teachers, you have a good relationship. They talk a lot about "tough love" and that describes how they manage things. Many think of the discipline but you understand why when you think of it in another way. It is about respect, tough love and discipline. We know that when we show the teachers respect, if we follow the rules, we know what we will get back. They are very good at giving rewards, they acknowledge those who need it. If you respect the teachers, you get it back 100 times.

Kim went to the school from years 6 to 9 and he sees Pascal as a central person for the school being the way it is. They have apparently had their differences but as time went on, this "tough love" left a strong impression on Kim. Today, when he is in senior high school, he says about Pascal:

> He is the one who has created the feeling of love at the school. It isn't just a workplace, it is also something more because of the person Pascal is. It has inspired me! If you feel good at your workplace, you do a better job. There aren't that many who do what he does but that is how I want my workplace to be in the future. At the same time, we have had our "moments"

says Kim and laughs.

Obviously, Pascal is a strong carrier and mediator of the culture at the school, so I felt I had to ask what his employees think would happen if he quit and someone else became principal; this is what Pieter Strijdom said:

> Our culture is strong, how would anyone be able to change it? I think that the staff would stop the new principal. Perhaps it is so, Barbara Bergström has obviously succeeded in affecting the culture in the entire school organisation even if there are different variations. There are examples of many business leaders and founders who have succeeded in creating a culture that lasts over time, as well as after their time, even if the nuances clearly change. Whatever would happen, I think there is a lot in what Pascal said in one of our interviews: "Culture has defined our success!"

"What do you mean by that?"

> The implementation of our culture and our values (ethos) is the foundation for our previous and future successes. Culture and our values define who you are and thus define your success or failure. If you build the wrong culture, you will not be able to deliver from the values you believe in. Culture and values go hand in hand when forming a company. We have some values that are central for us at IES and that we strongly believe in. We also have a local culture at IESS that is unique for us. For example, we don't take ourselves too seriously; we have fun together; and we joke—at the same time that we never forget what it is that drives us. This is one side of our culture. Another side is that we are hungry, we take up space, we move quickly and so on. Those are some examples of our culture and what defines us and our success.

"A culture of learning and development is rooted in values that support and encourage both organizational and human potential".[3] The right organisational culture is a success factor at the same time as it has a strong connection to values and the management model management by values (MBV) and has therefore earned its own chapter in this book. The strong and very recognisable culture that furthermore appears to last over time at Internationella Engelska Skolan Sundsvall is in large part a result of their work with values. MBV is however not just about the chance to have a new successful culture in your organisation. It makes the wish to create a dynamic culture possible, where employees engage in continuous learning, continuous improvement, recurring work with values, and introducing new employees into the culture. Dolan says that this dynamic requires one to leave a process of evaluation and instead monitor and review progress from "process of reviews" to "monitor progress".[4] This is needed to ensure that everyone is actually doing what they say they are doing. It sounds like something that could incite strong reactions in employees and as a sign that there is no trust between each other. But look again at Internationella Engelska Skolan Sundsvall and there is trust, as described by students, that teachers and staff know what is going on and react directly. This is what teachers mean when they say that there is always someone who knows when you come late or if for that matter you need help with something. Monitoring is possibly a negative sounding word but if used for the right purpose, it also creates a feeling of a fair system where everyone is treated equally. A safe system where you know that if something happens, you will get help but also a system that acknowledges what you do, good and bad. Dolan explains that there are some important things when monitoring is done: It must be "all inclusive", that is, no levels or areas are exempt from review; it must be open and transparent; it must be professional and at the same time sympathetic; it should not be perceived as a threat if deficiencies are detected but rather as an opportunity to solve misconceptions, to compensate for unforeseen problems, and to put more resources in areas one might have previously underestimated a need. To manage with MBV as a model isn't just about you making decisions on beliefs and formulating values; it is just as much about that you need to check that the results are consistent with the intentions and objectives. It wouldn't be enough for Internationella Engelska Skolan to have formulated their three core beliefs. They work everyday to evaluate that they are followed and challenge themselves to constantly have them in focus for their behaviour and to make decisions. For the evaluation of the values or culture to be accepted by the employees, they must all understand that it isn't for the leader's/boss's sake, but for everyone who stands behind the values and the articulated culture. Again, here I think of the clarity at Internationella Engelska Skolan if you are about to be employed or start as a student, you must confirm that you stand behind the values, you make the decision to participate.

Something else that is important, according to Dolan, is that the evaluation is transparent and that the result is communicated with everyone. This cannot be the job of a closed group. If the evaluation is perceived as control, or that the idea is to punish, then it loses its validity and the risk is high that the result will not be authentic and will show a skewed picture of the company's culture. During the months that I have continually met with him, Pascal has shown that he has a strong desire to talk to his staff, students and parents and even his boss about the results, and to together celebrate success and the present challenges for them. He often chooses to see the results as positive and to lift the school but turns the same results into a challenge to improve his own work; this is what the previous CEO for Internationella Engelska Skolan Ralph Riber said in an interview:

> When Pascal had a banner up saying that 99% of parents are satisfied, he talked to me about how he could try to reach the 1% that were not satisfied. I assert that, for the most part, the school has succeeded in having

unbelievable control over everything that happens without it feeling controlled. This is definitely something worth striving for and worth thinking about how they succeeded in doing this; the organisational culture they have created is surely a part of the answer.

In order to achieve a working organisational culture, Simon Dolan points out the importance of having a "common language".[5] It becomes a powerful circle where the language makes it possible for people to share values with each other, which creates a better understanding of the mutual values. Simple words such as respect or courage are interpreted differently by different people; in an organisation you need to know what they mean and what that means in practice. This is something one does at Internationella Engelska Skolan Sundsvall from accessing external information on the website to engaging in individual conversations about them. In an organisation, you need to present your values with a simple and precise language while at the same time provide definitions for each word. When you communicate in this way, you avoid misunderstandings about what the company's vision and values are.

What I have described in this chapter is what one could call a values-led culture, a culture that lives in the soft world. Let us put that in contrast with a more rational and economic culture, a culture that Dolan considers is doomed to fail. Leadership and the way to manage and lead during all of the 20th century has been characterised by controlling people's performance, rather than strengthening people's chances to perform; to reduce the costs rather than creating new ideas; and to produce rather than to sell. This is an inheritance from the industrial revolution that worked in that context but in today's society, people need something else. Even if leaders and leadership have of course evolved in the last one hundred years, we still have an inheritance that very much characterises our thoughts and views. Douglas McGregor (1957) formulated two early models of what motivates us at work and one of these is "Theory X",[6] which was based on traditional, rational and economic beliefs. See Figure 5.3.

In contrast to this, McGregor also presented his "Theory Y" which has more of a psychological and social dimension. In short, it is about how man can first reach their full potential when the job is meaningful and the person's own values and needs coincide with the company's objectives. We have seen in recent years that companies have begun

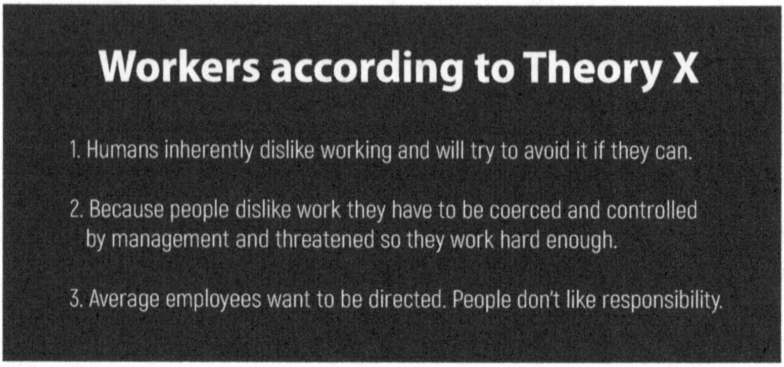

Workers according to Theory X

1. Humans inherently dislike working and will try to avoid it if they can.

2. Because people dislike work they have to be coerced and controlled by management and threatened so they work hard enough.

3. Average employees want to be directed. People don't like responsibility.

FIGURE 5.3
Founding convictions according to Theory X about what motivates us in the workplace. Ibid.

to change from control and bureaucracy to a management model that focuses on the development of the individual and of the organisation. According to Dolan, there is always a risk that one can find oneself in a ditch on one side or the other, most organisations find themselves in a landscape between Theory X and Theory Y. MBV is not about distancing oneself from different theories and models. MBV requires us to gather knowledge from what he has seen in history with what we know today to take us into the future:

> Organizations are constantly struggling to strike a balance between their control orientated culture and the development oriented culture. An overreliance on control and rational processes in the 21st century organisations contribute to an environment where employees are indifferent, uninspired and excessively dependent on leadership. The classical paradigms of management developed over the course of the 20th century are no longer effective; the bureaucratic model works only in limited environments and the socio-technical systems need more elements in order for it to work well.[7]

Companies and organisations that today successfully balance control and freedom to develop their organisation are worth spending time on, to understand the way of working behind it. The balance doesn't come with an answer sheet or a culture that one can copy but through systematic and conscious work. I am grateful that Pascal has chosen to share his story to increase understanding of the process. I will conclude this chapter with pictures that show how some value words have different meanings depending on if they are a part of the previously controlling management culture or a part of the new more development-based company culture. See Figures 5.4, 5.5, 5.6, 5.7, 5.8 and 5.9.

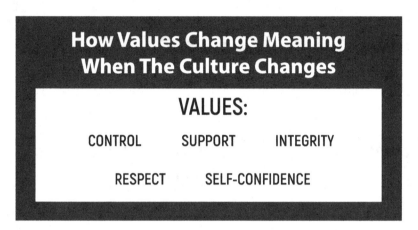

FIGURE 5.4
How values change meanings when the culture changes. This is described here from what company culture looked like in the 20th century compared to the 21st century, according to the writers of *Managing by Values*. Dolan, S. L., Garcia, S. and Richley, B. (2006). *Managing by Values, A Corporate Guide to Living, Being Alive, and Making a Living in the 21st Century*. London: Palgrave Macmillan, Page 80. Used with permission from Simon L. Dolan. Figure created by Norlins förlag.

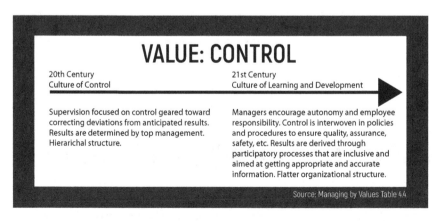

FIGURE 5.5
How the meaning of the word "control" has changed as a result of cultural change. Used with permission from Simon L. Dolan. Figure created by Norlins förlag.

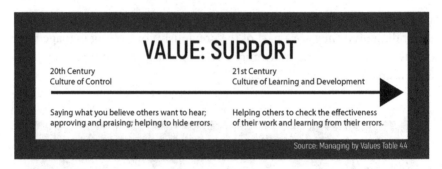

FIGURE 5.6
How the meaning of the word "support" has changed as a result of cultural change. Used with permission from Simon L. Dolan. Figure created by Norlins förlag.

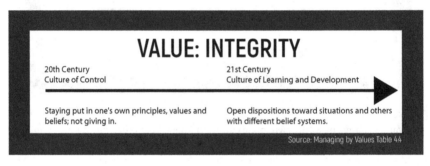

FIGURE 5.7
How the meaning of the word "integrity" has changed as a result of cultural change. Used with permission from Simon L. Dolan. Figure created by Norlins förlag.

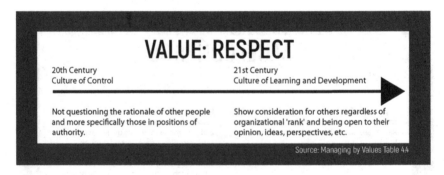

FIGURE 5.8
How the meaning of the word "respect" has changed as a result of cultural change. Used with permission from Simon L. Dolan. Figure created by Norlins förlag.

VALUE: SELF-CONFIDENCE

20th Century Culture of Control	21st Century Culture of Learning and Development
Demonstrating self-confidence through persuasion and 'winning'. Admission of errors is akin to 'losing face' and status. Posturing is a way of life.	Demonstrating self-confidence as well as accepting other opinions. Capacity to admit mistakes, learn from others regardless of position.

Source: Managing by Values Table 4.4

FIGURE 5.9
How the meaning of the word "self-confidence" has changed as a result of cultural change. Used with permission from Simon L. Dolan. Figure created by Norlins förlag.

NOTES

1. Cockerell, L. (2008). *Creating Magic: 10 Common Sense Leadership Strategies from a Life at Disney.* New York: Doubleday Publishing.
2. Internationella Engelska Skolan. Etiska riktlinjer för Internationella Engelska Skolan. https://engelska.se/sv/about-ies/ethical-guidelines (21 August 2017).
3. Dolan, S. L., Garcia, S. and Richley, B. (2006). *Managing by Values, A Corporate Guide to Living, Being Alive, and Making a Living in the 21st Century.* London: Palgrave Macmillan, Page 77.
4. Dolan, S. L., Garcia, S. and Richley, B. (2006). *Managing by Values, A Corporate Guide to Living, Being Alive, and Making a Living in the 21st Century.* London: Palgrave Macmillan, Page 195.
5. Dolan, S. L., Garcia, S. and Richley, B. (2006). *Managing by Values, A Corporate Guide to Living, Being Alive, and Making a Living in the 21st Century.* London: Palgrave Macmillan, Page 178.
6. McGregor, D.M. (1957). *The Human Side of Enterprise, Proceedings of the Fifth Anniversary Convocation of the School of Industrial Management.* Cambridge, MA: MIT Press. http://www.valuebasedmanagement.net/methods_mcgregor_theory_x_y.html.
7. Dolan, S. L., Garcia, S. and Richley, B. (2006). *Managing by Values, A Corporate Guide to Living, Being Alive, and Making a Living in the 21st Century.* London: Palgrave Macmillan, Page 94.

6

A True Leader?

I was given the possibility to be creative but this, unfortunately, required me to be a leader.

Pascal Brisson

Pascal is always well dressed…or perhaps not always. Sometimes in shorts and T-shirt covered in rainbow-coloured powder, sometimes dressed as a chicken or ferociously made up for Halloween, but mostly well dressed (Figure 6.1). Many talk about him as the principal in town who almost every morning stands outside the school and welcomes students. One can certainly discuss if Pascal Brisson is a good leader or not and it is interesting to ask oneself what the school would be like if someone else had taken the principal's position ten years ago. But I think that there is a lot in what Simon L. Dolan, Salvador Garcia and Bonnie Richley have written: "Behind every successful company—of whatever size or sector— there is a truly transformational leader, and a story of effective leadership to be told".[1]

"Was it obvious for you to become principal and be a leader?"

Pascal thinks a moment while he tries to remember how it was. He describes himself as a person who doesn't remember so much of what has been, his focus is constantly concentrated on what will happen in the future. But after a moment's careful consideration comes this answer:

"I saw an opportunity to create something and to do that, I needed to be principal".

Here there was room for him to be creative in an area where he felt at home, while at the same time, he could live his dream of creating a school.

FIGURE 6.1
Principal Pascal Brisson on stage together with the year 9s at Internationella Engelska Skolan Sundsvall at their graduation in 2017. Photo: Jody Thompson, Still Vision Photography.

> Everything that was on the internet was one thing, you could see Internationella Engelska Skolan's values, but I also saw how they had chosen to interpret the values and that was what was important. I could feel that this was a school I could stand behind 100%. There was also room for a principal to be independent and lead their own school, the power lies with the principal as long as you deliver what company management wants.

"It still sounds quite controlled how a school in this school organisation is run, how can you say that it gives opportunity to create?"

We are successful as a school because there is a clear idea about what the school will deliver from our values, there is no room to do anything other than just that. IES then allows each principal to design their school out of that, how you as a principal choose to deliver the school's ideas is up to you.

Pascal is clearly an appreciated leader in Internationella Engelska Skolan (IES). This is how Barbara Bergström expressed it:

"We in the company trust him. He is strong, trustworthy, honest and dedicated. These are excellent qualities for a leader".

Pascal is a leader who the organisation has chosen to invest in economically with large sums of money. These investments from IES in the school in Sundsvall are looking 20 years into the future.

> He is our success, and now is expanding with 360 students. The school in Sundsvall is among Sweden's top ten schools in size. It is quite fantastic that this is happening in Sundsvall which at its heart is a working-class town without a big academic tradition

says Ralph Riber.
"Why do you believe in him and Sundsvall?

> He always has drive. One time, he had a lot happening outside of the school because of illness of a person really close to him and he was still able to focus on the ongoing school expansion and the details around the renovations. I believe in his ability to implement it. This is also a way to meet his need for constant evolution.

Ralph met Pascal for the first time in late spring 2013. The first thing he noticed was the huge amount of energy Pascal has.

> He is like an idling engine in high gear. A lot of energy and difficulty sitting still. Engaged and passionate as a person and always observant. He is careful to highlight that he himself feels that he has an anxiety that in this context becomes something positive.

"In what way does he fit as a leader in your organisation?"

> He fits in the three cornerstones that Barbara Bergström stands for and that she has formulated: safety, focus on learning and to command the English language. It shows in his engagement in that everyone should feel safe and his desire to always be better in this area. The international perspective comes naturally with his multilingual background. Pascal personifies our values and lives them through his interpretation of them. It is a part of our culture that you want to put your own mark on things, be visible, present and switched on. He is a clear and present leader, just like our founder, Barbara Bergström. He doesn't hesitate, just like Barbara, to say what he is thinking. As her he keeps to his basic principles and basic values, and as he also likes to be at the centre.

In short, how would you summarise Pascal's leadership?

"All in, total engagement and a strong belief in what he does".

This chapter will focus on the person Pascal Brisson and his leadership. I see this as a leadership that is interesting to learn from. Not because we can or should be like him, but because it is through others' stories and experiences that we ourselves evolve and through that change for the better. In our society, we need to create room and opportunity for this type of leadership and I hope that this book provides the tools to do so. We need to have the right conditions for the future's leadership, a leadership that will hold over time in an increasingly complex world.

During Christmas break with his family in Canada, Pascal made his decision; he said yes to the principal's position in a whole new school. In two weeks, he went from a high school teacher to a leader in an as-yet-unknown organisation. He knew what they wanted him to deliver. The first thing after making this decision, what he had actually said yes to began to sink in. Once the first moment of panic was over, as he himself expressed it, he began to wonder what kind of leader and person he wanted to be in this new role.

> I read many books in order to find myself and I love to read and study leadership. I think a lot about who I am, look around and contemplate a lot back and forth. If there is something I am a fan of, it's Star Trek and Captain Jean-Luc Picard, an officer in Starfleet and amongst other things, known for his command on board the USS Enterprise-D and later Enterprise-E. He is focused, knows what he stands for and makes sure that everyone works with that as a starting point, at the same time he is as I am, not perfect. For example he doesn't have much patience (laughter). He is good at communicating and knows what needs to be communicated and makes sure that which should be said is said. This is something I try to do. He always challenges his team to help them to develop. We also do that at IESS. We allow people to be where they can do their best and develop. But perhaps the most important is that I don't take the safe before the unsafe, I take risks. Jean-Luc takes risks instead of taking the safe way. To have really good people around you, work hard, take risks but always ensure you don't lose focus on what you stand for. This defines Jean-Luc and that is what I try to be.

Pascal believes it took him almost two years before he in some way landed in what he wanted to be as a leader.

"It was a decision to be Pascal and that includes both the good and the bad. Of course there have been many mistakes that have resulted in that decision", he says and laughs but also with some seriousness.

For him it is about honesty and that is the only thing that works in the long run. At the same time, to be yourself isn't a constant, or as he expresses it:

"I am like clay, something that is constantly being shaped and at the same time is itself". See Figure 6.2.

On his desk there is always a stack of new books and on his office bookshelf are some of his favourite books, which is quite a lot, I might add. One of the first he read when he became principal was *Creating Magic* which is written by Lee Cockerell, a leader with over 20 years experience in the company Walt Disney. There seems to be a great deal of fascination around Walt Disney and their way of working. Assistant principal at Internationella Engelska Skolan Sundsvall (IESS), Petra Håkansson, told me how when Pascal had come back to school after being at Disney World with his family, there was a spark in his eyes as he told what he had experienced.

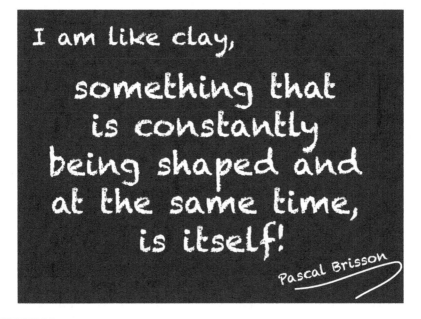

FIGURE 6.2
This is how Pascal described himself during one of our discussions in conjunction with working on this book.

"Petra, they are like us at Disney World, Mickey Mouse picks up trash!"

Clearly Pascal Brisson and Lee Cockerell are in agreement on at least one point; this is how Cockerell expresses it in his book *Creating Magic*: "Many people talk about having a business life and a personal life, but in reality you have only one life, and the best leaders are passionate about everything in it".[2]

The commitment is something many are witness to. It has become clear to me that Pascal is extremely aware of this. I think that he would be very surprised if he successfully surprised himself. This is why the discussion on what motivates and drives him is almost the basis of its own book, of which the title could be: Fear as a Positive Driving Force.

> I don't want to fail, this is something I got from my father. Fear is my driving force. Many would probably describe me as paranoid, I am driven by the fear of failing. This means that I am driven to find and see opportunities. The opposite of me would be someone driven by success. The irony with my drive, in contrast to if it were success, is that I am never done as you can always fail.

"But can you enjoy success?"

The answer which is often connected to yet another book he has read:

"You should read *The Wolf of Wall Street* by Jordan Belfort. I don't share his values but the book describes well how one can celebrate success. Of course we celebrate success at school!"

This was brought up by many colleagues that I interviewed, how an important part of their culture is that they celebrate success. When they got the statement from Skolinspektion in spring 2017, the whole school celebrated by putting up a huge banner that said: "Skolinspektion found no issues. You are of course one of the 6000 who are on the waiting list?" And all the students got ice cream. The concept is that success is celebrated together. But Pascal is never satisfied with success since this is not what drives him. Ralph Riber expressed this in the following:

"There is an anxiousness and perfectionism in that everyone should feel proud of the organisation. That anxiousness is the fuel in what he does".

Of that which drives and motivates Pascal, there is nothing specific that means the role of principal is more suitable for him than another leadership position. Many who I have spoken to have said that they think Pascal would be successful as a leader no matter the situation because he always puts in 100%. He himself feels that a large part of his motivation comes from the fact that it is a school.

> I love to work with children and feel at home in the school environment. Here, I do something for society and the time I invest builds something. For me it is important that I work for the community and not for the stock market. This justifies my 50+ hour work week.

Management by Values (MBV) provides tools for different dimensions of leadership. Basically, the purpose of these tools are: simplify, guide and secure commitment. Simplifying involves cutting through the organisational complexity created by the ever-increasing need to adapt to change at all levels in a company.

Guiding means channelling strategic vision towards the future.

Securing commitment involves translating the goals of strategic management into people policies designed to nurture employees' commitment to quality professional performance in their day-to-day work. MBV acknowledges that the essence of true leadership has always been marked by human values.[3]

TRANSFORMATIVE LEADER

In the beginning of this chapter the term transformational leader was used, a term that was introduced in 1978 by James MacGregor Burns.[4] According to Burns, transformational leadership is a process where leaders and followers help each other to a higher level in terms of morality and motivation. In *Beteendebloggen*[5] (the behaviour blog), Jakob Rådeborn has written about this form of leadership and this influence, impact, motivation, stimulus and care. He describes it like this:

> Transformational leaders are characterized by being appreciated by employees and seen as role models. These leaders have the ability to engage their followers and get them to follow the vision the leaders present. They have an ability to change employees attitudes and values in such a way that it contributes to the overall objective of the organization while the employees themselves develop. Much focus is in the future and emphasizes what is best for the organization and its members in the long term.

I see many of these characteristics in Pascal even if he himself has never talked about the term in our discussions.

There are four aspects that usually characterise a transformational leader. The first is **idealised influence**, which means that the leader is a role model for his/her employees from his/her values and moral compass. I don't know if Pascal will like me writing this, he is a little worried that I will describe him as the perfect person. For him, it is important to point out that just because you are values driven, it doesn't mean that you, as a person live up to only the good values. So, I just want to add here that Pascal isn't a thoroughly good person and is far from perfect in case I may have described him so. Now that I have cleared that up and surely calmed Pascal somewhat, I want to speak from my perspective. The clarity that Pascal has for which values apply and his ability to constantly associate them and act with them in the workplace makes him a role model. If he were not to act as he does, the team wouldn't either. He also builds trust through his own confidence in what the school stands for. Idealised influence also means that the leader acts in such a way that it benefits the organisation and the members, rather than the leader himself; there is no doubt that for Pascal, the school comes first. The second aspect is **inspirational motivation** and this relates to the leader delivering a vision that inspires, engages and motivates employees to follow. When I have talked with Simon L. Dolan, he has brought up the term "followership" instead of "leadership". This we-feeling at the school means that they move together. Pascal has successfully delivered the school's vision so that employees, students and parents want to agree. **Intellectual stimulus** is the third aspect. Here, employees are stimulated by new ideas and reflect over how the work is done. In this way, the leader contributes to developing the next generation of leaders. Even if the rules are there to be followed, I get the picture that there is constant discussion at the school, a discussion about how they can develop the school in the future but always with the same beliefs and starting point. I asked Petra Håkansson, Assistant Principal, how much Pascal gets involved with her or other leaders' work.

> We leaders are experienced enough that he has already made his mark on us before we become leaders. Pascal puts more time into those who are new or further down in the organisation. We in Team lead discuss with those who we feel have the correct competence for what we are wondering about and that doesn't have to be Pascal. Then, though it may not seem like it, Pascal is somewhat of a 'lone wolf"

says Petra.

The presence of intellectual stimulus at the school has been seen through my interviews with different employees and it is a central reason for why they are comfortable in the workplace. It has also meant that employees have stayed longer than they planned but also been the reason they come back if they have previously chosen to leave the school. The last aspect of transformational leadership is **individual care**. The leader should be responsive to employees' needs, show empathy and give support. This is something that has hit me about how Pascal sees his and his leadership team's role, their main task being to support teachers so they can do a good job. The focus is to ensure that a comfortable working environment, high academic standard, security and English should be made possible in the classroom. An example of his care is the personal letters he writes to his employees every Christmas break. To see the individual students and staff has characterised the school from that first meeting at Pascal's house where the leadership team pointed it out like a bright beacon. To see the individual is something he still brings up as one of the keys to a good school.

CHANGE LEADERS

In the book *Managing by Values*, leadership is described like this: "Leadership can be defined as the capacity to influence others' behaviors so as to channel their efforts toward the achievement of new goals. And… values are an essential element for channelling such efforts".[6] Change leaders successfully incorporate all three value sets as described in MBV's triaxial model. Economic values are used at the organisational level. Ethical and emotional values are used throughout the organisation on all levels. Change leaders are not just needed in large organisational changes; I think that today there is a need for change leaders continuously in organisations as everything happens so quickly and things change at high speed. At the same time, there are sometimes major culture changes. The way I see it, it was a culture change that Pascal managed to achieve in the Swedish system. A culture that creates pride for the organisation, a culture that contributes to job satisfaction and high ambition, a culture that results in good health amongst the staff and a culture that promotes child and youth learning. He got the opportunity to begin from the beginning. To build something from scratch in many ways makes it easier to create a culture but he has now also shown that he has the ability to keep and develop the culture over time during a time of expansion.

For a leader who leads through values (MBV) in a process for cultural change, it is impossible to improvise; the change must be formed and developed. I want to explain briefly the areas that are of particular importance for how this development should look, according to the authors of *Managing by Values*:[7]

1. **Personal development**. The transformative leader needs to be trustworthy and therefore needs his/her and the organisation's values to be clear. The leader must defend and assume the values that the employees understand to be the driving force in the organisation. Characteristics like openness, honesty, integrity and trustworthiness are central. This requires maturity and a high level of tolerance for different situations. A leader can't be dependent on instructions and rules to cope with all situations or when they end up in vulnerable positions. The leader needs to be able to show confidence before insecurity and risks. Self-awareness, to be adaptable, have intuition, energy, communication skills and strength to stand up against pressure are necessary characteristics. The personality, from how one manages situations, is extremely important "A leader paralyzed by an excess of stress may block the entire change process in an organization".[8]

2. **Global vision**. A transformative leader needs to have a genuine interest in everything going on in the organisation. This interest is shown through talking to and listening to everyone. Through this, one gains knowledge of one's customers, suppliers and competitors in other industries or in other countries. The ability to develop and use good channels of communication is necessary to be able to manage things in the organisation but also what is happening around the world. Developing political skills and building professional and social networks are necessary for managing different situations. One needs to be "on top of things", that is, to have control over what is happening by having an overview of events to ensure that the employees' and organisation's values are in line with each other. The ability to visualise possible future scenarios from different starting points strengthens the chance of getting employees on board.

3. **Strengthening and developing collaborators**. The leader needs to bond with their employees emotionally in a way that encourages them to work hard to achieve change. This requires empathy and the capacity to understand things from your colleagues' different perspectives at the same time as you disseminate inspirational pictures of the future. The ability to see and develop the skill in employees to take their own actions and decisions. The simplest way of doing this is to be a good example yourself. To listen and give time as it is necessary to be able to formulate the values in such a way that they are meaningful for people in the organisation. If one as leader wants to make it possible for others to get results and succeed, then one must foster a climate of innovative thought, creativity and experimentation in one's closest team members and legitimise the view that mistakes are something we can learn from. Attempting to counteract tendencies towards expecting a perfect performance and that one is the main person for all important tasks, it is necessary to delegate in a way that strengthens the organisation. Finally, a transformative leader must know which are collected mutual values in the organisation from the employees' perspective and be able to formulate them clearly, enthusiastically and honestly. Today, it is virtually impossible for a leader to be able to manipulate the basic values. If all this was in an advertisement for another job as boss/leader/principal, most would feel overwhelmed. It is central to emphasise the word development because it is about the development of the leader and organisation and that is ongoing. When I look at Pascal and his leadership team's leadership today, I can give examples of every point above. This depends partly on who Pascal is as a person but above all because of the very conscious work on his own leadership.

We surely have different ways that we improve ourselves. For me right now it was the choice to write a book about an area where I want to improve and learn more about. At Internationella Engelska Skolan Sundsvall, there seems to be a generosity when it comes to professional development for teachers and staff. For example, some teachers had the opportunity to go to Spain recently and "shadow" teachers there. Even in this area, Pascal chooses to put time into analysis to make the right decision. The professional development must take the employees and school forward with the school's beliefs.

Pascal very rarely goes on courses himself even if he can be generous with the rest of us. His way to improve is by reading biographies about successful people and drawing conclusions from what he has read on how it can be used here at school.

Assistant Principal Petra Håkansson

His own professional development will automatically impact the organisation largely through his very engaged leadership.

"The interest in being seen in the organisation is strong and the high presence in the classroom, lunch hall and corridors is central. It shows that the leader is interested in what we do and what happens", believes Anna-Maria Allanius, Assistant Principal.

"We in Team lead must have as a focus: We will support teachers; we will help teachers to teach; and we will make sure that we offer the best learning environment", says Pieter.

VOICES ABOUT PASCAL AS A LEADER

During my interviews with different people, I have received several descriptions of who Pascal is as a leader. This is how Barbara Bergström, founder for IES, describes him.

"He is a humble and fantastic leader. He is strong, he takes care of the whole organisation and he knows how to respond to people".

I think that what she describes is similar to the way previous student Kim Åkerström expresses it when he describes his previous principal.

In earlier schools the principal was the one sitting in the office. Pascal walks around in the corridors and shows himself and talks with people. It shows that he is the principal, but not in such as way that you need to bow before him (laughter), you respect him. You know that he is a good person. Pascal has a tough side so students absolutely have respect for him and you don't want to fight with him. I have respect for him because he can put his foot down when it is needed. At the same time, he is a principal that is really there in different situations. Pascal could for example come and play basketball in the breaks. It grew a good relationship that was built on respect.

Kim has described for me that the strongest impression made is of the relationships at the school, which Pascal has fostered through his leadership. Petra Håkansson explained that sometimes he is a little too caring of the relationships and can therefore have difficulty taking a break on the weekend.

> If Pascal embarrasses himself or does something wrong, he doesn't like it. He often knows when he for example has behaved wrongly towards someone and then he will want to apologise immediately. It has happened that he had called employees on a Saturday to apologise while the person in question had planned to relax on the weekend and wait until Monday to discuss it. Pascal wants to take action immediately.

Pascal's ability to quickly solve things and his commitment also came up in my conversation with Ralph.

> Pascal is always awake, he wakes up at 4am (Pascal says 5:30) and goes to sleep late. He has a restlessness that he has learned to rein in. This restlessness comes with a risk that he will tire people out but he often succeeds in finding the balance. He brings people with him. Pascal is a person that likes to be in the centre and therefore chooses to bring others forward instead. The result is often that people are noticed together with him.

Colleague Pieter brings up Pascal's ability to make a lot happen while at the same time never silencing the values.

"He can make almost anything become a school subject! But he always tests the ideas so that they are in line with what our school stands for".

So, is Pascal therefore a true leader? Are there people and personalities that are more or less suitable for a leadership position? Is it possible to learn to be the right leader for a certain context? The story shows that IES in their recruiting knew what they were doing when they employed Pascal. They found a person who matched their company culture and who stood for their beliefs of what makes a good school. Pascal's energy and motivation are important parts of what makes his leadership successful. Pascal has in turn a leadership a level above him that see his need for freedom, creativity and constant motion. All people have characteristics that are and can be a hindrance when they find themselves in a leadership position, even Pascal. But the awareness of yourself as a person and the awareness of the situation you are in makes it possible for the right decision to be made and provides conditions for a culture of constant evolution. For an organisation to have this type of leadership that Pascal symbolises, there needs to be a clear organisational idea and the possibility for the leader to create in order to deliver that idea. I think that we need to offer more of these "leader environments", otherwise we will lose valuable leaders of our companies and society's development.

I conclude this chapter with words about leadership from Simon and Pascal. This is how a successful leader for our time is described by the writers of the book *Managing by Values*: "The successful manager of the 21st century knows that their primary function is to continuously create convergence between organizational goals and objectives and those of its stakeholders through the articulation of shared values".[9] To achieve this, however, requires courage, says Pascal Brisson.

"Leadership requires muscles. You must see the need to talk about values and not just talk about what must be produced. You must stand up and talk—Leadership requires courage".

NOTES

1. Dolan, S. L., Garcia, S. and Richley, B. (2006). *Managing by Values, A Corporate Guide to Living, Being Alive, and Making a Living in the 21st Century*. London: Palgrave Macmillan, Page 119.
2. Cockerell, L. (2008). *Creating Magic: 10 Common Sense Leadership Strategies from a Life at Disney*. New York: Doubleday Publishing.
3. Dolan, S. L., Garcia, S. and Richley, B. (2006). *Managing by Values, A Corporate Guide to Living, Being Alive, and Making a Living in the 21st Century*. London: Palgrave Macmillan, Page 4–6.
4. Burns, J. M. (1978). *Leadership*. New York: Harper and Row.
5. Beteendebloggen, Transformatoriskt ledarskap. Inflytande, motivation, stimulans och omtanke.(29 February 2016) Rådeborn, J. http://www.beteendebloggen.com/blogg/transformatoriskt-ledarskap-inflytande-motivation-stimulans-och-omtanke (14 July 2017).
6. Dolan, S. L., Garcia, S. and Richley. (2006). *Managing by Values, A Corporate Guide to Living, Being Alive, and Making a Living in the 21st Century*. London: Palgrave Macmillan, Page 120.
7. Dolan, S. L., Garcia, S. and Richley, B. (2006). *Managing by Values, A Corporate Guide to Living, Being Alive, and Making a Living in the 21st Century*. London: Palgrave Macmillan.

8. Dolan, S. L., Garcia, S. and Richley, B. (2006). *Managing by Values, A Corporate Guide to Living, Being Alive, and Making a Living in the 21st Century.* London: Palgrave Macmillan. Page 122.

9. Dolan, S. L., Garcia, S. and Richley, B. (2006). *Managing by Values, A Corporate Guide to Living, Being Alive, and Making a Living in the 21st Century.* London: Palgrave Macmillan, Page 77.

7

Creating the Team

Our chief want is someone who will inspire us to be what we know we could be.

Ralph Waldo Emerson

I'm on the platform waiting for the train one very early morning. Most people are like me, ready for a work meeting in the capital but you see how they are tired and longing for a few hours sleep during the journey. Suddenly, behind me I hear lots of laughter and loud voices. As they come closer, I hear that they are speaking English. It becomes impossible not to turn around. There are around 20 people and many of them are wearing jackets that say "Internationella Engelska Skolan Sundsvall". Even though it was a few years ago, I can still remember the feeling, the feeling was that this was a group that you wanted to be a part of. They radiated energy, joy, self-esteem and community. This chapter is about creating a sense of teammanship within an organisation. See Figure 7.1.

If we start with the company's core beliefs, we see how the ideas around creating the team had already begun there. Internationella Engelska Skolan (IES) has the text in their brochure: *Commanding English the key to the world*[1] with the subtitle: "The People Who Do It" (2017). In the brochure, Internationella Engelska Skolan shows who they believe are central to delivering their vision and core beliefs, the people in their organisation. The company's thoughts around recruitment and support for staff are also communicated. This is how "the people who do it" are described:

The success of a school rests in its people, their competence, determination, unity of purpose and passion for education.

FIGURE 7.1
Internationella Engelska Skolan points out that the people are the reason for the school's success. Source: www.engelska.se.

> **Strong school leadership**. We recruit dedicated principals who deeply believe in our ethos and who can implement what IES stands for. A good school starts with a strong principal, who can make all staff go in the same direction. The principal is to be constantly visible, welcoming students in the morning and throughout the school day, not hiding behind a desk. He/ she is to be attentive to details, thereby upholding respect for the school as an orderly and positive workplace.
>
> **Recruit excellent teachers from around the world**. We recruit superb English-speaking teachers from countries including the USA and UK as well as Canada, which produces world-class teachers in maths and science. Our teachers are to "go the extra mile". They enjoy a calm and stimulating work environment where they can flourish.
>
> **Help teachers to develop**. Our schools have an energetic and uplifting atmosphere, partly due to the mixture of international and Swedish teachers. Thanks to the size of the organisation, we can add many forms of teacher development.[2]

This formulation clarifies who the workplace suits. A person who recruits bosses, principals, teachers and other staff know what they should be looking for. A person looking for a job knows what is expected and what type of workplace it is. With a clear starting point and thought around what team one wants to build, it is of course easier to make the team one wants.

Initially, the school in Sundsvall had Pascal Brisson. He was then free to build his first team. He got to decide who would be a part of it and from that create a completely new organisation. The first key people were of course crucial for how the start was and that team lay the groundwork for the school that today continues to grow and evolve. A strong school leadership was personified through Pascal. Now I am going to tell you how he recruited his first employees. Many of them who were there from the beginning now have leadership roles at the school.

Jens Hall was the first person employed. He is Employee #1! Pascal and Jens had worked together at the SPIN programme at Sundsvall High School (a social sciences programme with an international focus where the working language was English).

> We had both recently had a child, so we had a little bit more in common because of that. I knew that Pascal had applied for the position of principal and when he got the job, I was on paternity leave and studied computer science at the same time. We had lunch and I was offered the chance to work at the school 20–25% in the beginning to help "sell the school" to get students for the school start in autumn.

Jens took the offer and when the school opened in the following autumn, he was responsible for student care and had some teaching hours. He remembers one particular moment when Barbara Bergström and her husband visited the school in Sundsvall:

> Barbara's husband took me to the side and suddenly I found myself in a spontaneous interview. He asked why I had chosen to work at the school and if I was good at English. For me, the international environment was part of the appeal in the beginning but I stayed only one year and then left for another school. When I came back again after three years to work as leader of the new student care team, it was much more about the values. The school stands for something I stand for. There is consensus; we have fun together; fellowship between teachers and we have a common view of education. But I didn't end up being in charge of student care

says Jens and laughs, "instead it was social sciences and today I also work with Swedish as a second language".

Here, Pascal interrupts the interview:

"It is important that we always see where our staff fit best. Competence must be matched with need".

If you have had anything to do with Internationella Engelska Skolan Sundsvall (IESS), you have most certainly met Karin Henriksson. She was an acquaintance of Pascal's and while they were riding in Vätternrundan (the world's largest bike race, around Lake Vättern), they talked about what a school should be like and there was a great deal of talk about values. After that, there was an interview.

It sounded both interesting and good. In the beginning, I worked half time in the kitchen and half time in reception. Today, I make sure that things work and take care of the details. My work is to continually improve and develop our routines and "how we do things". I am responsible for welcoming all new teachers in a good way, it is important for us that everyone feels welcome

says Karin and smiles.

The next person to be employed applied himself and that was Pieter Strijdom. If there is something most people remember, it seems to be what they were wearing during their interview; Karin had a denim skirt and when Pieter met Pascal for the first time, he was wearing beige shorts. They obviously understood the dress code quite quickly and that this was something important. In 2009, Pieter had just moved to Sweden and started his Swedish For Immigrants (SFI) course. He had heard that an English school would open nearby, was interested, and contacted Pascal for an interview.

> We talked a lot about if I was the right person for the school, did I fit into the concept? It was clear what kind of school Pascal wanted to create. I got to start anyway as a drama teacher and even work with communication.

"How was it to start at the school and have Pascal as a boss?"

> I will never forget that first summer. It was a warm summer and we had a lot of work to do moving furniture to get the school in order. Pascal forced me to be dressed up every day—in case a parent popped in!

Another that applied herself was Petra Håkansson, today Assistant Principal for the last seven years. She worked at Internationella Engelska Skolan Järfälla and had heard about a new school opening in Sundsvall. She was interested in applying and talked with her then principal about it.

The recommendation she got from her then principal was to be clear about what she wanted to work on, since she is a person with strong opinions and a will to lead. Pascal said quite simply: "Do you want to be a Swedish teacher or do you want greater responsibility?"

> When I had come to what I wanted, I contacted Pascal. I said "You need me!" But it took three tries before he said yes. I was also clear that I wasn't a quiet person. In the first year, I basically presented all the documents we needed to run a school. Pascal came from the high school world and was not familiar with Junior High or the company and that was something that I could bring. For example, I organised students' action plans and took everything we could need from Järfälla.

"You both seem to be strong personalities; how does that work?"

> He knows that I say what I think while at the same time he knows that I say it as I want what is best for the school. He knows my intentions and that is why it works. In daily work, we often run "two parallel races". Pascal trusts me and he has therefore given some parts for me to be responsible for. If I think about it, we actually almost never meet

says Petra and laughs.

Even if Pascal has strong anxiety about the possibility of failing and has a strong overview of everything that happens, Petra's description shows that he can trust someone and delegate and drop some of the control.

From his own Canadian background, the connection to his homeland was natural for Pascal when he was to build an international and bilingual school. One of the first teachers recruited from Canada was Jocelyn Beranger, today a teacher and in charge of the Heads of houses.

> I met Pascal for the first time at a job fair in Canada. He told me he was going to start a new school in Sweden and that sounded cool. When I came to Sundsvall, there were two people who showed me around. My first Friday evening out on the town made me wonder: What kind of town have I actually moved to? Pascal said that if I survived the weekend, I was guaranteed a job on Monday

says Jocelyn and laughs. "I thought that I would stay one or max two years, but today I can't imagine a better workplace as a teacher".

"What was the decider that meant you could see yourself leaving Canada and moving to a new town in a country you had never been to before? And not only that, to a school that didn't exist yet".

"In the interview, Pascal described the school and it sounded like it stood for everything I stand for and everything I feel makes a good school".

RECRUITMENT

It is of course a great advantage to be able to choose your own colleagues and employees. To be able to begin at the beginning and choose the right people for the team and then build on that. At the same time, it can be a challenge to know who you will need before the organisation is up and running. I have described how some of the previous recruitments at Internationella Engelska Skolan Sundsvall happened but I have also interviewed several employees to get a bigger picture. Here is how Pascal answered the question of what he was thinking when choosing his closest colleagues:

It needs to be people you trust, that have the same philosophy, and that are driven. Petra and I argue quite often but we know that we are there for each other and for the school and we want the same thing. The people I want allow for mistakes, are well organised and trustworthy. We look for our employees worldwide. I sell our concept to people that we want to recruit and in that way, they can be convinced of our idea or not. To find the right employees requires a lot of work. I try to find things in people and see what they are good at. I really try to see who the person is inside and then build from that.

I can see a challenge in succeeding with recruitment in an organisation undergoing major expansion. For each academic year, a large number of new teachers and other staff have had to be employed. I asked Petra what she thought had made it possible to grow so quickly and at the same time keep the basic concepts and achieve good results.

"We have been able to choose all our employees ourselves and Pascal has been involved in employing everyone".

Something that characterises the staff at Internationella Engelska Skolan Sundsvall is the diversity and here I don't mean just in regards to nationality, but even in regards to personality. Even if many have strong personalities with a lot of will and drive, Pascal strives to complement that with those who contribute to calm and reflection or something else that increases diversity.

"Calm people contribute with balance and work well with us, they are important for the whole".

If you look at the leadership team, you see that together they become one good whole and they are all very aware of what their own and others' strengths are and in turn what they need to get help from each other. During one of our conversations, I saw for maybe the first time a little more unsure expression from Pascal in response to one of my questions. He wanted to ensure that I got the absolute best answer.

"Gustaf is much better at these questions, you should talk to him! We in the leadership team are like parents you turn to depending on what support you need. We complement each other".

Another strong characteristic of good recruitment is a high number of interviews. In my interview with a group of employees, it was almost a competition to see who had gone to the most interviews; for many it was three to four. It meant that the process is something memorable and causes laughter for many afterwards. When the school plans to employ someone, they want to be sure. At recruitment, they prioritise putting in time to properly present the school, to get a good picture of the person and to see where in the organisation the person fits best.

"It requires time to test and see if the person fits. You also need to think about if the person will be a good complement to the staff in general. Recruitment is quite simply not a quick process", Pascal says.

If the person responsible for recruitment feels unsure about something, they usually get help from others, they want a "second opinion". Here again, they get help from different people depending on what they are unsure about. Sometimes Karin in administration is brought in to check in on them or sometimes someone else is asked to think about something specific.

"We interviewed a new person and Pascal thought that when they talked about values that the person looked bored. Then I also got to meet the person to see if I got the same feeling", says Pieter Strijdom.

The school has as one of its main characteristics a high academic standard and good teachers are what makes that happen. It can make someone think that their academic success or ability to teach would be important at recruitment but from what has been told, that isn't the main focus.

> What we try for is that half the interview is to present what we believe in and we actually talk very little about their teaching qualifications. It is the person's characteristics that is the decider. The school's values, culture and way of working need to agree with who the person is. For the employee to be happy, develop and get tasks that bring out the best in the person, the leadership team needs to get to know the person early on

says Pascal.

Finally, when it comes to recruitment, I see a strong success factor that is surely the most important one also brought up in the book *Managing by Values*: "A recruiting organization must have a clear idea of the values it is seeking in candidates".[3] Without Internationella Engelska Skolan's clear formulations about what is expected of staff; without Pascal believing in the school's core beliefs and values; or without his beliefs about what culture he wants to create—recruitment would be blind. Pascal and his employees wouldn't know who they are looking for and the person employed wouldn't know if it's the right job.

THE RIGHT PERSON IN THE RIGHT PLACE

After a person has been employed, the next step is to put the person in the right position from the organisation's perspective and that of the individual. Seeing both sides has been said to be one of Pascal's strengths. Employees in the organisation are used to changing positions as things are constantly changing. To change positions is also a part of how the school works to quite simply test what works best. I'm thinking here of Petra who after many discussions with Pascal got to be on the team that started the school. She had her own strong drive and she knew what she wanted and what she didn't want to work on. Her tasks at the school have changed many times and today she is, as previously mentioned, Assistant Principal. Petra brings up, in my interview with her, the importance of her being able to focus on what she burns for most at the school. To be able to work with what she is most passionate about has been important for her motivation and drive.

> I have always been passionate about Junior High as it is the toughest period in life and therefore where you can make the biggest difference. In the

autumn, I was contacted via social media by one of my first mentor students who at the time, you would call a real 'troublemaker'. Today, 14 years later, the student is studying to be a civil engineer at the Royal Institute of Technology in Stockholm. If I, for example, had been made responsible for upper elementary, I would have surely started to lose my drive. That my thoughts around what I want to work with have been listened to and have given results has meant that I am extremely satisfied at work. I don't have five-year plans, I do what makes me happy. I need to like my job and feel that it is valuable.

To get individuals to feel that they are in the right position and at the same time feel that they contribute towards what is best for all, is surely a good way to build a good team. I think that the continual dialogue that goes on means that you feel listened to and you get a picture of the whole and you as an individual are a part of this whole. Petra continues:

Pascal is good at bringing out people's strengths. I am going to work with years 6–9 for example and Anna-Maria is perfect for years 3–5. You get to be where you have your strengths. Gustaf who works with us now has a skill in analysis and he is responsible for that.

Petra believes that being able to see skills means existing staff are happy and it is also a good way to get competent employees.

CONSENSUS AND COMMUNITY

That staff from IESS on the train made an impression not just on me. Pieter and Jens talk about a morning when they took the 5am train to Stockholm. They started the train ride by buying some coffee and then sat at their places and drank coffee and talked and laughed. After a moment, one of the other passengers turned around and says: "Can you shut up!" They laugh as they tell it.

"Sometimes we have too much fun together!"

This community within the school has a lot to do with the culture which was described in Chapter Five. A strong community is created through laughter and having fun together. If you take it one step further, it is about being there for each other. There is a culture of helping.

"When a person has started here, we support that person as much as we can, it is our greatest strength". says Pascal.

> We talk a lot to each other and for teachers, this becomes a natural segway into watching each others' lessons and giving feedback to each other. If I for example feel that there is a lot of noise in my lessons, I can ask a colleague to come and listen. I get help while at the same time what the students expect of us is more homogenous and it makes it more clear what level is expected, no matter which classroom they find themselves in

says Jocelyn.

When you are there, you are also a part of the team. The meetings for staff on Monday morning is something that is brought up by many in interviews. Jocelyn continues and says:

"The staff appreciate Monday morning because it means that everyone is on the same page".

At these meetings, Pascal always puts a lot of weight on values. He feels that having a consensus about them is the most important thing for everyone to be able to do a good job during the week.

> We are a strong team here at the school and we know each other well. This means that sometimes we know in advance and can figure out how for example Pascal is going to act and how he thinks—even if he doesn't know himself

says Petra and smiles.

PARTICIPATION

At a school, the team is bigger than just the staff; it is also the students and their families. In a discussion with a previous student from IESS, this participation is something he brought up. He means that as a student, he was already allowed to take an active position in the beginning and that students are included in different ways such as arranging different things:

> When I started at the school, I had to sign a lot of things and I liked that as it means I knew what was expected of me right from the start. The school also had us students participate in a good way, for example, it is the student council that arranged Anti-Bullying week, that made us active and

interested. In addition, we get the message more when we join in. The students participate in the school's work in different ways

says Kim Åkerström.

Petra talks about how in the autumn they need to increase their staff in administration.

> The employees know that we in Team Lead decide and implement a change but they have had the chance to participate in writing the work descriptions that we have used to help us write what we want. We make the decision in the end but it is an important success factor that they are a part of the process.

Participation at IESS builds on the idea that everyone takes part in discussions before different decisions. When the decision is made, it is expected that everyone goes towards the same goal and does what is decided. Even if the process towards the decision is good, the wrong decision can of course be made. Sometimes the issue is in the process itself. Petra continues:

> Sometimes the wrong decision is made but we have no problem with changing it. I had a meeting with several teachers and they had opinions about a decision that they didn't think was good at all. During the discussion, I sent a text message to Pascal: "They are not happy" and we immediately decided to take back the decision and talk about it again. If we want, we can make quick decisions but also make quick new ones when needed.

At the school they have a parent teacher organisation (PTA). Three parents from each class are representatives and approximately twice per term, there is a meeting where at least one of these three are expected to participate. The goal with the organisation is to create a strong connection between guardians and the school and through this organise meetings and activities. They want to support IESS in their work to help students achieve their goals. It is the parents who run this and the engagement is appreciated by the school. For example, at graduations, a representative from the PTA gives out prizes to the students.

"We want to involve the parents so they will in turn invest in the school with time and commitment", says Pascal.

The school stands for their values and decisions. To create legitimacy and commitment to these, they work for involvement and participation.

UNLEARNING

As much as the journey to creating a sense of teammanship is about learning and taking on values, it is also about unlearning existing values, a concept that Simon L. Dolan uses. This is important when bigger cultural changes occur but is also an important perspective when employing new staff. We all have our own values about how we behave at work and privately from our own experiences. If you want to make a team, you need to work on identifying what the people have brought with them and what needs to be learned. I brought up this perspective with Pascal to hear how he works with this:

"As a new employee, you get to see many documents before you start that we go through in the first week. When they start, they get a mentor that follows and coaches them".

Pascal sees that many bring with them a certain way of working and that can be difficult to change.

"Some of what they have learned won't work with us; we must therefore show how a change can help them as individuals and then it usually is easier to drop old habits.

"You have a large number of people from other countries, mostly Canada, is there something in particular they often have to relearn?"

We want the school to be bilingual and our English-speaking teachers don't always see the importance of this. They can think it is enough with English. There are a few different arguments that usually work. Sometimes I say it is a part of Swedish law; that probably is the least effective for bringing a change. They of course often have a commitment to the students, so I usually say that the students need the Swedish to be able to succeed in high school after they leave us. The most effective way to get them to understand is to convince them that the lessons will flow much better. I usually explain that they will be able to work better and faster. We people need to see the value for ourselves—there is a strong driving force in being willing to change your own attitude.

Pascal also sees the need to get the students at the school to go through the process of relearning. They come from different contexts and different schools and bring with them their own pattern and understandings.

> When it comes to students, there are very often concrete things that they need to unlearn and accept, such as not running in the corridors and our rules for mobile phones. For this to be possible, we need to explain why the rules are good for them.

In the book *Managing by Values*, there is a strong focus on what is needed for a cultural change and they have written very well about what is needed for such a change process. Amongst other things, what is needed to find and choose the right people to lead change is described. I think that every organisation can find themselves in constant culture change or in a defence of culture position. The connection between culture and making the right team for the organisation is strong. According to Management by Values (MBV), the whole organisation needs to be anchored in the kind of culture desired. The anchoring needs to come from the highest leadership. The leaders need to be involved. An environment that is values driven is described like this: "MBV espouses values that recognize the potential of everyone to make a contribution based on their knowledge and experience, and that mutual learning is not constrained by notions of up, down or sideways, in a dynamic and open organization".[4] In the twentieth century, we have seen a change amongst company leadership. Leaders begin to more and more drop an old culture where the top is best. According to Dolan, they begin to realise more and more that predictions and recipes from experts are not as valid or effective as having a creative vision that is shared by everyone in the organisation. To achieve this, taking part is central and in turn requires leaders/people who are interested in the culture question and gets others to feel involved. This confirms Pascal's choice to put a lot of time and energy into recruitment and having the right person in the right place: "The manager's task is to identify those showing the most interest and commitment, and incorporating them into the change dialogue, so that their contributions can be constructively considered".[5] Participation contributes in the short term to a good communicative environment and counteracts resistance to change. In the long term, it creates a culture of participation where everyone feels engaged and dedicated to the success of the organisation and each other.

In 1985, Michael Porter, in his book *Competitive Advantage: Creating and Sustaining Superior Performance* presented the value chain: a model for analysing specific activities through which companies can create value and competitive advantages. A way to understand customers need structures and through that develop the company in a profitable way. Dolan believes that the most important part of a company's value chain is to reflect upon the mutual values in the organisation. If mutual values are missing, the company's value chain is harmed.[6] If you are going to make and build a team, you need to find the weak links in the chain and strengthen them. Ask yourself: Where are the weak links in my organisation? How does this affect/is affected by the values?

At Internationella Engelska Skolan Sundsvall, which has now been running for nine years, they stand before new challenges in making the team. They are good at recruitment but how should they keep the current inspiration and motivation amongst the staff who have stayed within the organisation for a long time?

"We are talking about that right now,[7] how we will keep the spark in everyone. Our staff are driven people and does everyone need the opportunity to take the next step to deliver in the long term?"

Petra asks this question in my conversation with her and she sees this as a new challenge for the school. Pascal also sees this and has therefore chosen to go back to basics in a particular way and prioritises the school's beliefs and values.

"Pascal, what are you most proud of today?"

"We have well educated, strong and very different people but everyone works towards a common and clear goal. We walk together!"

He has apparently succeeded in creating his team, I hope that you have been able to find some tools to make yours. Let us end this chapter with a quote from Pascal on why the subject of the team is important in a book about leadership:

"Leadership isn't about a person, everything we have accomplished is built on us".

NOTES

1. Internationella Engelska Skolan. Commanding English the key to the world. https ://engelska.se/sites/default/files/IES%20Brochure%20Oct%202016web.pdf (17 July 2017).
2. Internationella Engelska Skolan. Commanding English the key to the world. https ://engelska.se/sites/default/files/IES%20Brochure%20Oct%202016web.pdf (17 July 2017).
3. Dolan, S. L., Garcia, S. and Rickely. (2006). *Managing by Values, A Corporate Guide to Living, Being Alive, and Making a Living in the 21st Century.* London: Palgrave Macmillan, Page 189.
4. Dolan, S. L., Garcia, S. and Richley, B. (2006). *Managing by Values, A Corporate Guide to Living, Being Alive, and Making a Living in the 21st Century.* London: Palgrave Macmillan, Page 158.
5. Dolan, S. L., Garcia, S. and Richley, B. (2006). *Managing by Values, A Corporate Guide to Living, Being Alive, and Making a Living in the 21st Century.* London: Palgrave Macmillan, Page 158.
6. Dolan, S. L. (2011). *Coaching by Values.* iUniverse, Pages 82–83.
7. Additional note: In June 2018 the International English School in Sundsvall presented a new plan. As the school turned ten years old they will continue to focus on the basics but they also want to make bigger impact on society and the community. They are aiming at becoming a hub of knowledge on how to run a school. All staff will be offered the possibility of organising workshops and seminars and to invite other schools to participate. It is believed that these two initiatives willl make the city and country even stronger while at the same time injecting energy in their staff that have been with them for many years.

8

Do We Need Visions and Missions When We Have Values?

The strategic vision may be considered as nothing more complicated than the optimistic projection of a desirable future.[1]

S. Dolan, S. Garcia, B. Richley

In a book about leadership and organisational management, it is impossible to skip the concepts of vision and mission. It is however not something that has been given a lot of space in my conversations with Pascal. At the school, it is their three beliefs, principles or values, yes, loved children have many names, that are in focus. The question I have come to ask myself is: Are visions and missions needed when one builds an organisation on values?

A short answer to my question is: "MBV in three words means: alignment between core values, the organisation's mission and its future vision".[2] What MBV does is suggest a conceptual approach to facilitating strategic actions by showing the difference between vision and mission and strategic and operative values. The vision, mission and operative values are considered to be the company's constitutional core.[3]

A vision, or perhaps even a common vision, can be defined in the following way:

The creation of a collective mental image of the values integrated in the vision of the future towards which the company wants to go, in the medium to long term (5–10 years), the decision to create the capability to reach this future, and the courage to believe in this future.[4]

If, as a leader, you want to get others to follow, you need to present the way for today and for the future. A voiced vision is an expression of the organisation's potential. If the vision is going to deserve its place, it is not enough that the owners are satisfied with how it is expressed; it is important that as many as possible on all levels of the organisation have enthusiasm and commitment to it. When a leader presents the vision, it should inspire in such a way that it legitimises everyone's efforts needed to reach the expressed ambition.

> Our vision and our view of life is something we share with parents, students and new staff. Each year, all staff sign a document with the vision on it. It also says how we do things and what we have come to agree on here at school

explains Pascal.

To talk about the future and where you are heading is the first step of course but for it to be meaningful, you need to excite enthusiasm. Obviously, Pascal has succeeded with this because he has managed to get the team to work towards the same goal. I think that part of this depends on his ability to visualise and explain with words. He adds to this often with lots of energy, seriousness and humour.

"I have a very clear picture of how I want things to be", says Pascal.

This must make things easier as a leader, you need to have your own clear picture to be able to communicate it and then enthusiastic people want to work for it. Even if the leader has a clear picture of their goal or vision and is good at communicating it, this is not enough. Pascal continues.

> Many want to plan but often no one wants to talk about what you want to create, they would rather do things. This has become clear to me during my ten years as principal of the school. It has therefore required courage from my side that we take time to discuss if we are going to reach the goal or vision. It is easy to say what you want to be and which values you want but then slowing down, talking about it and reflecting over it requires courage from leaders.

Pascal's way of working as a leader strengthens his above words. A vision isn't just making a future picture; it is just as much about the decision to achieve that vision and the courage to believe in it. When the leader lives up to this and gets employees to follow and it becomes a natural part of the daily work and the daily discussions, then it becomes a powerful tool.

Another more practical dimension is how to formulate a good vision. I don't know how many situations I have found myself in where we have sat and discussed words backwards, forwards and upside down. However, we did not do this starting from the company's or the organisation's core values. According to the book *Managing by Values* the following is needed for a good vision: "The vision needs to be sufficiently ambitious to excite enthusiasm, sufficiently comprehensive to embrace everyone, sufficiently consistent to be meaningful, yet sufficiently realistic to assure the shareholders that their investment will be profitable".[5] This is shown in the challenge of creating a vision that applies to many who have different interests. At the same time as it does apply to many, it must stay true to the organisation's shared values. Without a doubt, the authors consider the preparation and consolidation of a clear and attractive vision about where the company is going as crucial to linking the strategic elements with the psychological elements in individuals in the organisation. If you don't have a clear vision about the future, this is shown in a leadership that lacks authority. Pascal talks about what they have thought about in terms of vision for the school in Sundsvall.

> In the beginning, our dream, that is, our vision, was to grow so we could have our own facilities for our entire operation, like for example Physical Education and health. We have also wanted to offer our organisation to more students the whole time because we believe that it is good for Sundsvall. Another example for our work with vision, but that has a more short-term perspective, is that we look back on what has happened in the past year, every year. This means that we can identify what we want to do better—to then be able to decide how we are going to do that. This gives us visions that are close to us, and in that way help us with the long-term vision. We have had the courage to do the things that ensure that we will reach our vision.

If a vision is an image of the future of the organisation, a mission is why the organisation exists. You can't have a vision if you don't know why you need it. A company's mission should have two different components; one being economic and the other being social.[6] It needs to both explicitly express and yet also have the potential to be reformulated according to how the organisation develops. The success of the economic part of the mission enables the social part to exist, regardless of whether this has been intentional or not.[7] In the book *Managing by Values*, some of the values that are possible in the two parts are exemplified. Economic values in the mission can be profit, efficiency, benefits, satisfied shareholders, wealth or as high a return on investments as possible. Social values can be both for the organisation as a whole or for a specific activity or a specific part of the company. Here are some examples: Create jobs, increase the quality of living, contribute to society, to entertain, to communicate, to educate, or to cure. To formulate and communicate the mission creates a feeling of pride and belonging to the organisation; this motivates a person's commitment and effort and provides security for customers who pay for the company's products or services.[8] See Figure 8.1.

In the process of formulating and bringing up the organisation's mission, there are some questions we recommend asking:[9]

1. Who are the company's owners and what do they expect of the company in the long and short term?

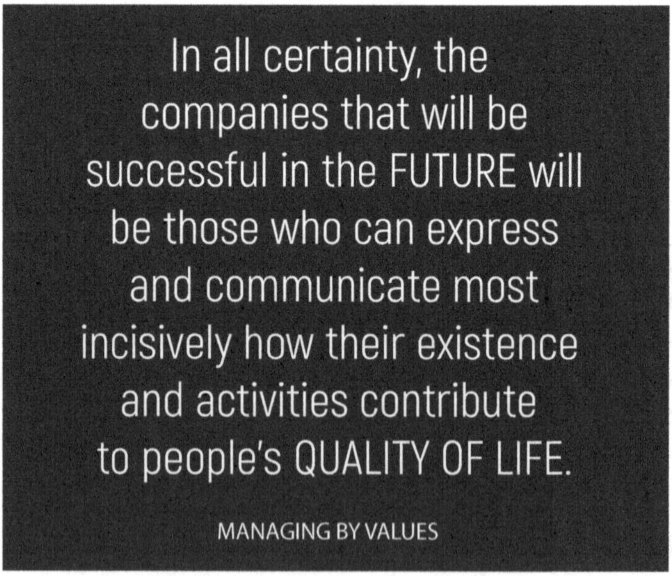

In all certainty, the companies that will be successful in the FUTURE will be those who can express and communicate most incisively how their existence and activities contribute to people's QUALITY OF LIFE.

MANAGING BY VALUES

FIGURE 8.1
Simon L. Dolan believes contribution to quality of life is essential for companies to be successful in the future. Source: *Managing by Values*. Dolan, S. L., Garcia, S. and Richley, B. (2006). *Managing by Values, A Corporate Guide to Living, Being Alive, and Making a Living in the 21st Century*. London: Palgrave Macmillan, Page 165.

2. What is it that your company does really well, better than others? What is it that the company really contributes to society?
3. What is it that customers and users of the company's products or services really need from the company? What is it that really makes them feel satisfaction (happiness, security, knowledge or status)?
4. What can the organisation really and realistically give staff?
5. What can the organisation offer their stakeholders?

Again, it is necessary to include the whole organisation in the strategic work for it to be successful. It is complex but all perspectives need to be included. When the mission is to be communicated, it should be done in different ways depending on if the information is external or internal. In external communication, it can be more general and not as clearly connected to the daily work that is carried out internally in the organisation. If the same mission is to have a real meaning for those employed, it needs to be connected to specific job descriptions and purposes.

Initially, this chapter described three parts that according to MBV, are considered to be parts of an organisation's core, namely vision, mission and operative values.[10] Even if another chapter in this book has been about values as a concept, it is interesting in this situation to talk about the concept of final values and operating values. This shows how values have meaning on both a strategic and operative level. The company's final values are a part of the vision for the future and the mission which answers the question of why it exists. These values can be described as the company's goal that together creates a validity around the mutual values. When we as an organisation have come to where we want to go and why we do it, then this also needs to be noticed in the daily activities on all levels. The values that characterise how we do the job and that create culture are called operative values. These are values that people often see as the most useful and important to being able to reach those final values, the final goal. The next step in the strategic work is bringing forward principles to help guide the collective efforts in the best way to enable the achievement of the wished-for future. The principles are also needed to enable the operative values being accepted as the foundation of the organisation's culture.

This is quite a short description of something complex but hopefully you have some ideas to take with you into your own situation. To make the theory more practical, I have chosen to look at Internationella Engelska Skolan's (IES's) work with this. I haven't analysed their strategic processes but have used the information they have published externally. When it comes to more strategic questions, it isn't just a single principal, or in this case Pascal, who is responsible. His part is that he wholeheartedly embraced the concept and strategy enough to be able to deliver from it in his daily work. The leader of the school in Sundsvall, through his active and conscious efforts, ensures that Internationella Engelska Skolan's strategic work is the guide for joint efforts to achieve their goals.

When I went to find the school group's vision, mission operative values and principles I was at first a bit confused. The three pillars popped up a little bit here and there and everything felt the same and it became difficult to know what was what. Again, I want to point out that this is my analysis of the school and not something they themselves have been a part of. The story in this book is about Pascal but to understand his leadership, the context he is in is central. When it comes to Internationella Engelska Skolan, Pascal is clear that everything has its beginning with the founder Barbara Bergström; it is she who has formulated and formed what the school was in the beginning and what it is today.

From IES's website and public documents, my interpretation of their vision is the following: "Where teachers can teach and students can learn". If you are going to then analyse this from previous reasoning in this chapter, you can ask yourself if it successfully balances building enthusiasm and at the same time includes enough realism. The vision should also include all areas in the organisation. In one way, you can think that this vision should be obvious for a school and in this way makes the vision perhaps pointless. At the same time, it briefly summarises what a school is about, what is absolutely the most basic for the organisation. If this doesn't work, then the rest isn't really worth much. Put the vision in the societal context and it becomes more relevant since this workplace environment for teachers and students isn't always a given in other schools in Sweden.

They called their mission "What we stand for",[11] and here you get the answer to why the company exists. They want to teach children to command the English language and to provide a safe and orderly school environment while at the same time having high academic expectations and ambitions. Here, they also elaborate on why this is important. They then take the vision and mission to a more operative level with the next title: "What we do".[12] Here, they have the same three points as they have under the mission but they explain how they do them. It describes how they have rules for an orderly environment that are signed by students and parents. They also explain how the staff make it possible to achieve what the school promises. All of this together with their ethical guidelines make it very clear where they want to go with the organisation, how they want to get there and how it is today. If this is not delivered, there are clear instructions for how they should react.

Something that strikes me when I look at the strategic work of this school group based on the MBV perspective is that my first feeling of ambiguity was completely reversed. The extreme clarity and unity in everything the school does makes it difficult to draw clear lines between the different strategic levels. All the discussions Pascal and I have had about the school's three pillars to work out if they are values, beliefs, principles or culture now begin to be clearer. Sometimes I have thought that the school has missed some strategic step or some level. Sometimes I have come to the conclusion that it is still values they are talking about. What IES do and have done is ensure that everything is welded together. Everything they do operatively or strategically is grounded in those initial beliefs that the founder once formulated. This strong connection makes the organisation extremely powerful and clear. Here, they do exactly what was initially described in this chapter that MBV is about—connect core values, mission and vision. When members of an organisation together agree (it isn't enough to just decide) on the values, mission and vision, then you can achieve success together and develop and build from what happens in more and more complex surroundings.

When Pascal received the question about the school's vision and strategic work, he answered:

> That is the whole reason our school is successful. We communicate it when we recruit teachers from Canada, we talk about it at every weekly meeting, it is something we believe in, we sign that we know what is expected at every salary and personal development talk. We understand the vision and connect it to what it means for the individual. If you are clear and honest, it will be successful. You can't pretend, it has to be true. This defines who we are. When we don't deliver, we know about it because everyone knows what is expected of us. This is the core of our success.

NOTES

1. Dolan, S. L., Garcia, S. and Richely, B. (2006). *Managing by Values, A Corporate Guide to Living, Being Alive and Making a Living in the 21st Century*. London: Palgrave Macmillian, Page 143.

2. Dolan, S. L., Garcia, S. and Richley, B. (2006). *Managing by Values, A Corporate Guide to Living, Being Alive, and Making a Living in the 21st Century.* London: Palgrave Macmillan, Page 198.
3. Ibid., Page 155.
4. Ibid., Page 159.
5. Ibid., Page 161.
6. Ibid., Page 164.
7. Ibid., Page 164.
8. Ibid., Page 165.
9. Ibid., Page 166.
10. Ibid., Page 170.
11. Internationella Engelska Skolan. What we stand for. https://engelska.se/sv/about-ies/what-we-stand (23 July 2017).
12. Internationella Engelska Skolan. What we do. https://engelska.se/sv/about-ies/what-we-do (23 July 2017).

9

The Importance of the Right Conditions

Teachers are kings and queens, the rest of us are here to support them. If we fail here then the students, the most important people in a school, will never succeed.

Pascal Brisson

We can all do something good from whatever situation we are in. However, having the right conditions is a great enabler. From a leadership perspective, I realise that the right conditions are needed for leaders to be their best. For a successful organisation, each leader must give employees the right conditions to achieve the vision. Just as much as we need to encourage each other to do what we can where we are, we need to encourage the creation of environments that make sustainable leadership possible. When Pascal comes into a situation where the values agree with him and there is a balance between control and freedom to be creative and feel secure, something can happen. His personal success as a leader is built on who he is but also on the conditions he has been given. This chapter is about what made his leadership possible but also what in his leadership provides the conditions for his employees to together build a successful organisation.

BEING IN THE RIGHT PLACE

"Values are not only words. Values guide and direct our behavior and affect our daily experiences".[1] If you agree with this, that means our values have a strong impact on our everyday lives. We often talk about culture clashes but seldom about values clashes. Culture clashes come up in many different situations and aren't just connected to nationality. What is expected of you in the break room at work? Is it part of the culture to talk with everyone or do people sit in different groups? Just how you are supposed to behave in the break room is a culture. This in turn has been made through the mutual values at the company. If you sit in the wrong place or say hello in a way other than what is expected, you go against the culture. If you start a discussion and want to start changing the culture, you will surely come to a values clash. Clashes don't need to be something negative or troublesome however, it of course depends on your attitude. But the need to fit in is important for us. You are perhaps like me and want to take the chance to say or do something unexpected just to get a reaction and are quite happy to "swim against the current". But of course, we still feel best when we feel that everyone around us has some kind of common view. You know when you meet people that you suddenly "click with", that feeling of being on the same page, that is a good feeling. Dolan uses a metaphor in his book *Coaching by Values*[2] which is about shoes—if the shoe fits, use the shoes, if it doesn't, don't. He uses the metaphor from two perspectives; one of them is about the importance of values for you to be happy. He believes that if your values don't agree with the values of your partner, your organisation, your surroundings, yes even your country, you are going to have the feeling of not fitting in. In the long run, this will have consequences that mean you will feel psychologically worse and in the end actually be in physical pain.[3] It is normal that we humans look for a culture that feels right for us, an environment where our values agree completely or almost completely with us. You as a leader need to find a place where the shoes, that is you, fit in. When you employ people, do you look for employees who will fit into the culture and agree with the values or do you try to force the shoes on them until they get a dead toenail? Or perhaps you think that the foot can have a gap in the shoe while it grows a few sizes? To make it even more complicated, it is true of course, that we sometimes need to change shoes. They have worked for a while but then you need a new pair. It can be that the company changes the values or that you choose to change jobs. I think that maybe the values are the most important factor for the right conditions for leaders and all employees. Pascal applied and took the job as principal for a new school mainly because he shared their values.

"I really felt that here I could build a school I can believe in".

That first feeling has meant that he has continued to believe in the school he leads in Sundsvall. His and the school's values are still in line with each other and mean he is really satisfied at and with the job. The time and commitment that is put into finding the right employees is so that they will feel the same thing as Pascal—I'm in the right place. Pascal as a leader has also understood the importance in making sure there are common values so that those employed can be happy, to strengthen the team and to achieve good results. From every perspective, it is advantageous that we humans are in a place that is right for us, as Fernando Savater expresses it: "You can live according to all kinds of systems, but there are some systems that don't let you live".[4]

PRACTICALITIES

Let us leave soft values as a tool for making the right conditions. In all branches, there is of course an understanding of how things should be done and which template fits best. Personally, I am one of those who talked about how small classes and smaller schools give students and teachers the best conditions. This I have thought with good intentions of course, that I want each child to be seen and from there, develop. That is why I asked the question to Pascal, as I understand I am not the only one who wonders, how they as a school look at the number of students in classes. A class at Internationella Engelska Skolan Sundsvall often has 32 students. The question is, can this create the right conditions for teachers to have the energy to do a good job? Are these the right conditions for students to achieve good results while at the same time feeling safe, which are two guiding principles at the school? Pascal seems to be used to this question and says that the big classes provide conditions to have more support, support that is more specifically adapted to need. My question actually becomes pointless since the school shows such good results, good emotional and mental health amongst staff and very satisfied parents. The other question about the size of the school being an issue has been asked of Pascal, not just because the school has gone from being a smaller school to soon being one of the largest schools in Sweden.

"Can a school be unlimited in size and still work? Can it still be faithful to its values?" I wonder.

There must be a breaking point… or no actually not. If you go to university, it works. Of course, it can be a problem but if you see and worry about the problems and from that change structures and work constantly, it is possible. If you're not worried, there is a risk in growing. A solution that I see is to divide the school into two different physical units so that it has the feeling of a smaller school.

In a complex environment like a school, and with so many opinions from different directions, the conditions for teachers are important for them to be able to contribute to and achieve the goals and visions. Each teacher becomes, one could say, a leader for different teams of students. In discussion with teachers at the school, Anna-Maria explains in practical terms what she thinks is an important condition for her:

Here there are routines and therefore you know what is expected. For example, it is clear how a parent evening should work so you don't need to put any time or energy into thinking about it. There is a support structure in the organisation with many different support mechanisms. We are good at helping each other

RELATIONSHIPS, TO BE SEEN AND TO FEEL SECURE

"The environment that simultaneously focuses on a high quality of performance and a high quality of life realizes that these conditions arise from a good psychological relationship between the individual and the organization as a whole".[5] In discussions with different teachers and people who are team leads at the school, you notice colleagues who are extremely warm towards each other and a strong loyalty to the organisation. Of course, it happens that they argue over things and have their conflicts, but it is more of the nature that one can experience in a family than one that is built in a situation of competition and fear. Kim Åkerström, a previous student at the school, tells how he recently participated in saying goodbye and thanking some teachers, something that happens on the last day for teachers after the students finish for the year. There, he saw the warmth between colleagues and the good relationships between the school and the people who work there.

A lot of it is because Pascal does so much more than what he needs to do. When he thanked some of the teachers that were leaving, I was so touched even though I had no relationship with them. He has built a feeling of love at the school.

In my first interview with Pascal, he took up and emphasised the importance of seeing the individual, whether it be an employee or student. This has been important from the start and is emphasised today. He sees the challenge now that it is a bigger school and he personally will not be able to see everyone in one go. During one of my interviews with him, he gets a text message on his phone. He apologises as he needs to answer. After a few more messages, he says:

You have to excuse me, I have to go out a moment and help with something.

It was Friday afternoon and someone on staff was sad for some reason. He came back after just a few minutes.

The person needed a hug, now we can continue.

I have many positive experiences of leaders but of course also have examples of leaders that I feel should work differently. Pascal as a leader for his staff is as he wants teachers to be towards students; he practices "tough love". A deep commitment to each person, a willingness to help and support with love while at the same time it is clear what is expected and what the consequences are if decisions are not followed. Mattias Nilsson moved from Stockholm to Sundsvall to work at the school. After five years, he quit but then asked to come back and is once again employed at the school.

There has been a vacuum for two years, the principal at the school didn't visit my classroom once!

The constant presence of leaders in an organisation can of course be experienced as stressful and as some form of surveillance. A continual check that "I am doing it right and am delivering what I should". But what we can see in Internationella Engelska Skolan Sundsvall (IESS) as an organisation is that this has a competitive advantage. If you have had a chance to be a part of an active and engaged leadership, to be seen as co-workers, you miss the day that it disappears. I talked with a student who was quite new to the school. The student loved the school but there was one subject and one teacher where it wasn't working as well as in other things. In the discussion, we tried to understand what the difference was and after a moment, the student came up with the answer:

> This teacher doesn't see me as a person like the others do.

With this example, I don't want to call out any particular teacher but want to show how a well-functioning system works. A new student and a relatively young person without any deep understandings of the organisation's strategies and values can quite quickly notice when something is different. The student noticed something that Pascal and the leadership team decided nine years ago was one of the most important things at the school and still is. This makes the example fantastic, I think. We all make mistakes and in all organisations, it happens that we sometimes miss the goal and purpose in our day-to-day work. But what is amazing and I think noteworthy is that it is noticed when someone doesn't deliver the basic values. Then you have succeeded! Then the system is self regulating. If we call the student a customer, then here the customer has noticed something that doesn't mesh with what the company usually delivers. This suggests to me that in 99% of cases, the staff at school see students as individuals and they have therefore succeeded in their work with values. It also says to me that the values are clear for the customer because they react when they are not delivered.

To be seen and to have good relationships at your workplace creates security. At the school, there is a structured system for working with feeling safe through investigations that study where and when someone feels insecure or worried. Based on this, action is taken to increase the feeling of safety. At the same time, according to employees I have spoken with, there is a continual dialogue about safety. Leaders have a continual dialogue with teachers about whether they feel safe or insecure so that they can act quickly. When the investigations are done, they don't want to be surprised by the result but instead want to know what is going on in the normal daily work. The question of security has during recent years, gathered different dimensions, especially in schools. In Sweden, we're used to schools being an open environment, quite free from threats. The questions surrounding security are today strongly characterised by preventative measures and routines in case something unexpected happens. In order to have an organisation where employees are able to work to the best of their abilities, they need to feel safe; safety being both on the psychosocial plane and the physical environment they are in. Internationella Engelska Skolan Sundsvall has been exposed to threat. When I came to one of my interviews with Pascal, the police were still at the school and one armed police officer was still in his office. They needed to debrief after the day's events and despite the tough day, the room was calm and both parties felt satisfied with their work together. I had of course said we could do the interview another day but he is extremely loyal towards what he has decided with others, so putting my interview off was out of the question; I think this says something about Pascal. I want to talk about this incident because it shows a leadership that can survive a complex situation. Pascal is obviously deeply concerned about the development we see of threats to schools and the terrible examples of violence that we see around Sweden and the rest of the world. But this late afternoon, I met a quite satisfied leader, he could now breathe out and note that when the unexpected happens, everything works as planned. Surely his drive, powered by anxiety, had minimised the risks.

> Everyone knew exactly what needed to be done. When the police came, I could tell them exactly where all students and staff were and how many there were.

Ralph Riber, previous CEO of Internationella Engelska Skolan (IES), described it like so in his interview:

> Pascal has a great ability to create awareness about what he does from different angles. When it comes to threats towards the school and how he manages them, this is an example that shows that. He got the school, police, the task force leader and teachers to work together in an exemplary way.

He also tells how he sees fear as a driving force:

"Fear in the right doses is not paralysing fear, it means that you can act". Pascal prepares constantly. He doesn't wait until Skolinspektion comes to act. Anxiety, in the right amount, is very much part of his leadership which

FIGURE 9.1
Pascal in a meeting in his office, dressed as a chicken. Photo: Jody Thompson, Still Vision Photography.

leads to a constant need to drive things forward. In some organisations, there is a fear of doing something wrong which results in people not daring to do anything—neither make a decision nor act—it isn't like that at IESS.

There is a feeling of being able to trust in the system and know that the leadership can survive when the challenges are at their greatest. That creates a feeling of security and creates conditions to be able to release control of what you are not personally responsible for. This provides the conditions that enable doing a really good job. See Figure 9.1.

COMMUNICATION AND PARTICIPATION

In all relationships, groups and organisations, communication is the prerequisite for accomplishing something together. When the organisation grows and gets bigger and bigger, there is greater need for focus on how the communication is carried out. According to the writers of *Managing by Values*, communication is: "the only tool we possess to achieve the 'miracle' of authentic change".[6] Even if this book in its guidance about communication is focused mainly on what is needed when a company is going through a culture change, good communication is still central to maintaining the culture you are happy with. Good communication provides the conditions for efficiency. In your organisation, you can manage employees either by force or free will, which it will be is decided on the way you communicate. If you are in an expansion phase and growing, it is important to keep the channels of communication open between leaders and employees.

At the beginning of the 20th century, it worked quite well to just send information from leadership to those employed to get the job done and the business would be successful. Today, good communication is two-way communication to build engagement. If you don't succeed in building engagement, the risk is great that it sends a signal that the company doesn't see the individual as a fundamental factor in the organisation. In such an environment, it is difficult to get along with employees, so it is important to build a common culture, the employee's own development and effective internal communication. Here, it is interesting to see Pascal who is a very communicative leader, this being an element of his personality:

"He has a great ability to communicate and is always at the front and participating in the debate", explains Ralph.

The school wouldn't have been so big if those who had chosen to talk with Pascal had not done that. As they have grown, he has delegated responsibility; the same goes for communication. Here there are challenges for the leadership team to discuss. Even if there are two assistant principals, the principal is the primary leader with the most responsibility and often the one that employees want to reach. This has been especially clear with those employees who have been there a longer time and are used to that. At the school, they need to find a new way to work and prioritise as it isn't practical for Pascal to do things in the same way now that there are over 125 employees as opposed to when there was 25.

The communication needs to be persuasive both in a logical and emotional way according to Management by Values (MBV).[7] If you listened to or spoke with Pascal, you would see that this is one of his strengths. He is himself is convinced of what he wants to achieve and he can tell a really good story which is good when needing to communicate. There is a fine line between being persuasive and being manipulative and it must be honest communication and not internal advertising. If there is something Pascal has contributed as a leader which has provided conditions for the school's success, it is his ability to balance that. He says himself that he hates being a salesman. It was one of the more disliked parts of his job as principal, when he had to ring around to "sell the school" to parents.

He uses a lot of what Dolan describes as persuasive communication: "Persuasion in this sense has more to do with clarity and logic, with sincerity and the proper expression of values, goals and the individual's roles related to their capabilities".[8] Pascal often uses facts and statistics and formulates it with emotion and clarity when he communicates. Values, as you probably have realised by now, are constantly a part of his leadership and communication. He knows where he and the school are going and is able to make others follow. As described earlier in this chapter, he puts a lot of energy into making every individual see their part in the organisation and to contribute and develop in the best way. What he has had the ability to do is to also communicate how everyone should communicate so it doesn't stop with him.

"I have had meetings with parents and students about what we stand for at the school. Then teachers do the same thing with their students".

"How do you work on communication?"

> We get better all the time but we have always seen communication as extremely important. Sometimes this has led to us over communicating. All of our communication should be clearly connected to our three core beliefs about safety and order, high academic expectations and the English language. This isn't so easy to teach everyone but we work a lot with how we answer emails or express ourselves when we send information. I want that when we communicate, we always talk about what we believe in and how we will deliver that.

During the few months when I followed Pascal's work and through our discussions, I saw a leader that cares a lot about being able to communicate with his staff. This isn't something he does because he must or because it is needed, rather he longs to be able to talk about things, whether he must apologise or tell that the school managed to get no criticisms from Skolinspektionen. The right internal conditions mean you as a leader have enough information, this is something Pascal makes sure he has, if it doesn't come naturally, and that employees are a part of the communication. The external communication provides the conditions for having satisfied customers and for creating a positive image of the business.

"We have succeeded in having the image we have and here, communication has been important".

RESOURCES

Everyone in team lead roles at Internationella Engelska Skolan Sundsvall shows in their attitude that they are there to support and enable teachers to do a good job. The organisation makes sure that there are routines and rules that ease daily work, sees to it that there is psychosocial support when it is needed, coaching in how teaching can improve and is an active part of making an environment where teachers can spend their time simply teaching possible. For this to be possible, team leaders must be competent and able to promote the right culture and values. This is something Pascal and his colleagues have seen and therefore put energy into building a leadership that has dimensions according to need, that complements each other and that is clearly anchored in values. Assistant Principal Petra Håkansson explains:

"We have built on leadership as a whole to strengthen the management team. In the Fall (2017) we are going to have an Academic Manager full time for the first time".

An indication that an organisation is complex is that there are many people involved both in what must be done and even on what is offered based on who uses the product or service. This is one of the reasons for why a school is a good example of complex organisation. When it comes to resources, human capital is a crucial resource for having the potential to build a strong, successful and long-term sustainable organisation. The fact that Pascal has clearly chosen an individual focus is favourable to people, the human capital are happy, feel good and deliver. To invest time, commitment and support in the organisation's most important resource provides results. To be able to do this it of course requires will and courage. When you engage in human relationships, a communicative openness and values management, courage is needed as you cannot duck or hide as a leader. Even if a lot is possible and has gone well for the school, Pascal often takes up that they soon might fail and maybe won't be successful at all. Perhaps his greatest worry is that he will make a mistake that will negatively affect the school. The prerequisites for a leader to be able to act based on will and courage has of course to do with personality, personal characteristics and knowledge. But it is also built on the fact that the organisation he finds himself in allows him to do that.

To be able to put energy into human capital, economic resources are also needed. Organisations in the public sector with a lot of human capital have for many years been characterised by the fact that it's savings that matter. I often wonder what it would be like to constantly work in an organisation where the fear of budget cuts and the feeling that "I cost too much" is part of my day. If budgets being met that is the most important management tool that one could fail to reach year after year, you would experience confusion between wanting to be enough for your users, patients or students and at the same time saving money. It is relevant to ask if there is a correlation between resource shortage and increasing ill health. Then one can ask whether is it lack of resources or poor use of resources—what of that is connected to poor leadership? My answer would be most of it is connected to this. Let us leave the public sector and go back to the school in Sundsvall. As I wrote earlier in this chapter, the average number of students in the classroom here is 32 and it isn't that the school has decided that 32 students create the ultimate teaching environment, this is connected to economic resources. To have a good economy where you can afford good facilities, activities, material, professional development and extra staff that support teachers and students, there needs to be some optimisation somewhere. The decision was made that 32 students is possible if the right support is given and it also provides economic stability. In my conversations with Pascal, the leadership team, teachers and students, people have almost never spoken about money. I haven't led the conversation there, either. What everyone is aware of and what Pascal communicates, is that if they don't have any students, they have no income and no jobs. But there isn't a focus on that "we do a good job so we get money"; instead the focus is on delivering what was promised through their beliefs. I still have expected to hear a comment from somewhere "if we just had the money, we could…" but that never came up. Dolan, Garcia and Richley believe that one condition for management by values is that you should ask yourself: "Do we have the necessary resources? What resources will we need?"[9] and you have answers to those questions. An organisation with their economy in order where you know that it is managed in such a way that you don't need to worry about sudden changes, provides security. The focus for leaders and employees becomes not about counting money but about delivering values. I think this motivates and contributes to good health.

EXPECTATIONS

Do you have the conditions to do a good job, or do it at all, if you don't know what is expected? Of course, we can all try to figure out what is expected, and if successful in doing so use that knowledge to do a fantastic job. From an organisational perspective, this isn't sustainable; it builds on the individual's ability to guess rather than leadership. When Pascal said yes to the position of principal, he knew what his bosses expected of him. They were careful not to just inform him of what was expected but also wanted to ensure that he had understood. Through this, he felt security in knowing he was in the right place and what he had to do in order to deliver.

The creativity came in figuring out the how. Even if the expectations are clear from the company level when it comes to their expectations of their principals, they have on top of that a continual dialogue:

> We have a dialogue all the time but Pascal as a leader appreciates his autonomy so that is important for him. From the IES management's perspective, we don't look at details, we just ensure that he delivers a sustainable school that follows our values

explains Ralph Riber.

I also asked Pascal how much he is expected to take his decisions upwards in the organisation.

> I am allowed to be quite free and this is allowed because I deliver a product that mirrors our values. My father was a so-called hockey parent and he pushed me hard and that has made me a person who delivers but it is under the condition that I can decide myself. I don't want someone to tell me how I should work, there is always conflict in me to deliver what is expected and at the same time, decide for myself. When I have to make a decision, I usually think: "Is this good for the organisation?"

"What is your relationship like with the CEO of the company?

> Our CEO has seen and understood that I am an entrepreneur that likes to be creative and therefore knows that if they were to limit me, they would lose me. I call them sometimes to see how far I can push things or to debate

questions on a more strategic level. We never call each other to talk about how I run the school. They can challenge me and I them. There must be people like me but I can be quite difficult to work with.

What expectations are there for the staff that Pascal employs? Here we can connect again to the recruitment process that was described in Chapter Seven where a lot of time was put into what was expected first and foremost from a values perspective. Each year, every teacher must sign a quite comprehensive document, "Basic Defining Policy Documents", where they read what the school stands for, what the schools in the IES do, what the conditions for a good learning environment are, and the ethical guidelines for IES. It is difficult to work at the school and not know what is expected since they are very careful to avoid that from happening. The challenge with expectations in this context could be that they are set on the highest level and it is perceived as being too demanding for employees. I therefore asked Pascal what he does if his employees fail at living up to expectations.

> It depends on why they failed. If you don't want to do what is expected, then perhaps this isn't the right workplace. If you have tried and failed, then I and your team lead make sure you get the help you need to do better in the future.

Pascal is careful to follow this up in his organisation through constant communication, through sharing information and through being present in the organisation. He does this above and beyond what is expected of him explains Ralph.

> For us as an organisation, it is important that people are responsible for the values being followed. It isn't micromanagement but all employees must sign that they know what is expected. Pascal has chosen to make things clearer in the classroom and has clear expectations on how teachers should act.

"At the school in Sundsvall, all teachers start their lessons in the same way, we have a common structure for that", explains Pascal.

Expressed expectations create clarity on all levels. It helps make priorities clearer in whichever area you as a person can be creative and create. For each organisation, you need to think about how much and in what way you communicate expectations. From a leadership perspective, this is something that you need to put time into and it needs to be a part of the strategic work. For MBV to work, there is a strong connection to the fact that one also must expect values to make an impression on the whole organisation.

MEANINGFUL

When all the strategies are in place, in the end it is about how the daily work is understood and feels. MBV "aims to achieve high performance in day-to-day work making it more meaningful".[10] It is exactly the meaningfulness that makes Pascal every day and every week put his soul into his job as principal of the school. He describes it himself how he has a greater responsibility to society, to give children and youths a really good school life and that makes his efforts meaningful. In his communication with teachers, other staff, students and parents he often describes what the point of what you do in school is. If there wasn't any meaning in something, then it would have no value. Perhaps it is this anchoring in meaningfulness that makes many do their best no matter if it is Pascal or a student that is tired of school.

With this chapter, I wanted to show that good leadership or a successful organisation doesn't just depend on individuals' ability to take initiative or competence. All humans feel better and perform better when they get the right conditions.

NOTES

1. Dolan, S. L., Garcia, S. and Richley, B. (2006). *Managing by Values, A Corporate Guide to Living, Being Alive, and Making a Living in the 21st Century*. London: Palgrave Macmillan, Page 27.
2. Simon L. Dolan. (2011). *Coaching by Values*. iUniverse, Page 93.
3. Ibid., Page 125.
4. Dolan, S. L., Garcia, S. and Richley, B. (2006). *Managing by Values, A Corporate Guide to Living, Being Alive, and Making a Living in the 21st Century*. London: Palgrave Macmillan, Page 27.
5. Ibid., Page 104.

6. Ibid., Page 134.
7. Ibid., Page 135.
8. Ibid., Page 135.
9. Ibid., Page 149.
10. Ibid., Page 22.

10

Control, Trust and Meatballs

If you do not set an example of openness, you will not be trusted; if you're not trusted, you won't have credibility; if you don't have credibility, you will not have influence; and if you don't have influence, you'll be a leader in title only.

Lee Cockerell[1]

One question that I have wrestled with a lot is the balance between control and trust in others. Our world shows greater suspicion and more control amongst other things as a consequence of terrorists which attack innocent people in countries at peace. I have a feeling that even Swedish society goes towards more and more control rather than trust. In government, it is about internal controls, the potential to follow up and accountability. *Sveriges kommuner och landsting* (SKL, Swedish Association of Local Authorities and Regions) says the following about performance management on their website: Controlling results or so called results management aims to move the perspective of goal management from resources and activities to results that are achieved in the organisation's service to the user. In short—the quality and service citizens get for their tax money. Here, this management model from the 1960s is still defended but they try to refine it by changing goals, so they are no longer about resources and activities, but are about which results they want to achieve instead. In my work with municipal budgets, I am used to us politicians trying to educate ourselves away from the bike-shed effect and instead move towards impact goals, that is, the results we want to achieve, rather than specific tasks. (For example, if the task is to build two swimming pools, the impact goal might be to give a greater number of citizens access to swimming facilities.) I think we have gone in the wrong direction. Instead of going to the beginning of what affects the outcome, one chooses to directly control the outcome. Of course, we should have visions and goals but they will not be achieved without clear anchoring in values and beliefs. Here, Internationella Engelska Skolan (IES) and Pascal show brave leadership. When guidelines for management of a public organisation is to steer towards results, IES doesn't abandon their model but instead continues to lead with beliefs and values. This doesn't mean that I think it is wrong to use *Open comparisons*[2] which is a good tool for municipalities to be able to compare their organisations. It is very good for benchmarking and worldwide analysis especially in the public sector where competition isn't a natural part of their organisation. But it is wrong when the results of these comparisons are used, instead of being seen as a basis for development, to strive to be "Sweden's best school". Of course many are triggered to be the best but the question is how long can this motivation last when you aren't in that position. Compare it to being driven to deliver a safe school environment for all students—this makes coming to work even more meaningful. What drives an organisation must be achievable and at the same time something that means one is never done.

I think now is a good time to tell a story that they talk about at IES Sundsvall they call the "meatball incident". Some have only heard about it, others were there and can tell the story from different perspectives. I have chosen ex-student Kim Åkerström's perspective. This happened some years ago. There was one week left until summer break and the students who were in year 9 had begun to feel creative. The wanted to do something that would be remembered after they had graduated and a big prank was planned. Everyone was fully aware that there could be consequences but creativity took over. Some students took on the leader role but it was spread to all the students in year 9. Together, they decided that it would happen in the lunch hall and a food fight was planned. The students planned that it would happen on the day when all the year 9s ate lunch at the same time to have the biggest effect. It was a Tuesday. That day, they served meatballs, mini sausages and macaroni. One of the classes was a little bit more mischievous than the others and they sat in a corner of the lunch hall.

"Principal Brisson was in the lunch hall to keep an eye on that mischievous class and the rest of us just sat there and waited for him to go so we could start the food fight", tells Kim. Everyone knew what would happen but there were only a few who dared.

> When Pascal had in the end left the lunch hall, one boy jumped up and threw a meatball. Then I stood up and threw a meatball. The peer pressure made us do what we knew was wrong. The food fight lasted maybe 10 seconds before teachers, staff and Pascal stopped us.

"What were the consequences?"

"A really angry Pascal. He took this very hard. He was disappointed and hurt. First he reacted with pure anger and was going to cancel the school prom and everything but quite quickly, he became more professional".

"Yes so how was what happened managed?"

> Pascal went directly to his office and wrote an email to all the parents. He wrote that he thought it was very sad what had happened and that he was hurt. He also gathered all the year nines in the gym and said that it absolutely was not OK and anyone who knew who was involved or how it happened was to come to him directly. After that were there many individual meetings with me and others.

"What do you remember most from the incident?"

> That Pascal was disappointed, we had a good relationship and then this happens in my last days at the school. His disappointment hurt me. We got to go to prom and celebrate graduating as planned and we can joke about it today but I still have guilty feelings.

The story shows that the organisation has clear rules and works strongly with values and good relationships so if someone in the organisation decides to do the wrong thing, they know it is wrong. This time it was teenagers with a summer break feeling but there are many reasons that people might want to test and break against what is expected and right even as an adult in different situations. The students knew that it wouldn't go unnoticed and that there would be consequences. There was also a control system in place. Kim tells how there was a good relationship in the school with the staff there but peer pressure was stronger anyway. Even when both control and trust is there, this cannot protect against someone or several people consciously doing something wrong. I think about what happens when something has gone wrong; it can have an impact on the future of the organisation. One could see this as an innocent prank by some teens. They could have cleaned up after themselves, been told off, then continued as usual. Here there were feelings of full commitment from the principal and staff. Parents were to be informed and everything was investigated to the smallest detail. Pascal, staff and students describe it today as not being about the food fight but about a betrayal of trust and that was more painful and serious. The conclusion that everyone made is only possible to see in a context where values are highest on the agenda.

> It was still cool to see the guys' reactions after the incident, they sat in my office and cried because they knew that they had broken something that the school stood for. They quickly saw that what they had done was against our values. When you have made a mistake, it is important to see that we have chosen to react strongly. If we had not acted after, it would have been a bigger mistake

says Pascal when he reflects over the incident some years later.

Internationella Engelska Skolan, as you have surely noticed, has many guiding principles and quite tight control over the fact that everyone in the organisation must live up to the guiding principles. Furthermore, the school in Sundsvall appears to be a school within the company group where they would rather control more than less. I think that this is interesting to reflect over since Pascal describes himself as a person and leader who needs freedom and the opportunity to be able to create and be creative himself. Ralph explains control in the following way:

"Structure and boundaries are underappreciated for creativity. We have succeeded not because we have 20 different schools in one school but because everyone follows the recipe. Everyone must sign up for our values".

I also asked Pascal how he sees the balance between leading his organisation with rules and/or values.

> Google says that they have a free working environment but there is a lot that is already decided there. A school environment without rules means uncertainty. You need to feel secure to be able to be creative. If you are worrying, you are focusing on something else. Rules are needed to create a structure that makes it possible for people to be creative.

Earlier in the book, we have thought about how management has vision and knowledge about most things that happen. We have also looked at the importance of participation. These things are of course relevant to finding the right balance in an organisation between how much should be controlled and how much should be based on trust in shared values in order to guarantee that regulations and routines are followed. There is a lot written about this chapter's subject in the book *Managing by Values* which is a good tool for you as a leader when you are weighing things up. To be able to solve the dilemma between security and risk as well as between control and development is essential for survival and growth for a company. What MBV presents is somewhat of a new thing to management theory. Most frameworks and models lean towards either more bureaucratic and formal organisations or towards a more humanistic and sociotechnical model of an organisation. Instead of presenting a model for either control or development, they propose an integration between the two as a philosophy and as an application.

If an organisation is recognised too much for giving orders and wanting to have control, the result is that people lose vitality, engagement and drive. This can be devastating for companies as it often leads to the best staff getting tired of it, giving up and quitting. On the other side, there is also a risk that as a company you can trust too much in values of expansion and change. Then there is too much differentiation and too little specialisation; too many risks rather than secure routines; too much acquisition rather than investment; or too much new company areas instead of trying to be really good at your main skills. Even this can bring negative consequences. The result is the risk of an organisation becoming somewhat chaotic, which goes against engagement and creates a lack of identity. As in so many situations, there is no perfect and ultimate balance. There isn't even a static way of being; where the balance varies. The art lies in having a feeling for where you need to be on the scale right now, according to the context and situation. The writers have brought forward a model where you can calculate where on the scale in integration between expansion and concentration are.[3] You can get maximum 80 points and then you have scored highest on the scale for expansion in all areas. Also, you can get minimum minus 80 points and then you have scored highest on the scale for concentration. The point of the model is to show where things are lacking in each direction. If you get 80 or near that, there is a great risk that there is chaos in your organisation. If the result is close to minus 80, there is a great risk that you are leading in almost a military style and that employees will become tired of it and wonder why they are even in the company. Some examples of the different areas that are to be assessed are how undefined or defined the structures are; innovation versus administration; participation in or acceptance for decisions made; as well as process-oriented or results-oriented management. I don't know if you can easily assess those areas within your organisation and find a good balance by using this method but it can surely give a picture of where one is. It becomes a form of self assessment. What is good to take with you is that the balance between control and what I have chosen to call trust is difficult but needs to be constantly assessed to ensure sustainable leadership since the consequences are harmful if it swings too far in either direction.

Pascal is a visible and present leader that is driven by the fear that something will go wrong, and this results in a controlling leadership. I am surprised that many of his employees are characterised by drive and creativity when the organisation and he as a leader make so many decisions and control so much, the space for own initiative would then be perceived as limited. Many have the perception that IES in Sundsvall's success is because of their rules and authority but the question is if it really is that simple. I don't think so. I think it is because they have found the right balance between trust and rules for this specific organisation and that one is driven by the context one is in. In this balance, it is clear within which boundaries one can be innovative and creative. But I understand from Pascal that not everyone is always happy with his idea of what is the right balance.

> Some say that they think that I decide everything. I don't think that myself as I always try to check with others before I make a decision. If it were so that I always decided everything, I think this organisation would survive max two years. I usually often go around and ask people about different things and then I get lots of input for the decisions that must be made.

"But isn't it just your perception that you ask many and do you know how many of your employees see things?"

> I have a good example that shows how close my communication is with teachers. The school cooperates well with the unions. We meet once a month and they are a part of our Team Lead.[4] But I also have a close dialogue with our employees so it is rare that there is a big debate or discussion about employees' conditions. I work for a good dialogue with all parts.

"Do you think that you will be able to continue with this when the school gets even bigger?"

> We divide the organisation more between us in the leadership team and I can focus on 2–3 things. I am amongst other things, responsible for feedback to teachers. Now when there has been a lot with the school constructions and a lot of discussion with the municipality, I haven't had the time I would have liked when it comes to following up with the staff members and giving them the attention they deserve.

"Have you noticed that the staff have noticed this?

> Every Christmas, I usually write a personal letter to each staff member. Before Christmas 2016, I had so much to do plus a close member of my family was very sick and there was no letter for the first time since I opened the school. Some staff were really sad and I saw the value the letter has.

"What did you learn from that?

> That staff need contact with their principal. Therefore it feels good that we are getting another assistant principal as it will allow me to be even more present. After the reactions I got, I chose to try and correct my mistake and therefore wrote a summer letter. It really hit me how they valued contact with me. I wonder if I have built a sustainable system? I think I have done this but it requires me to be well organised and prioritise right. I have said to everyone that we all must find a way to connect, an own system where they can get the feedback they need. Can they build other channels for follow up? The organisation has become very dependent on me as I have been involved in everything all the time

says Pascal.

In the middle of Pascal's quest to find mistakes; coming up with ideas about how things can be solved; and his speed in solving things himself it feels as though his employees can smile a little at his way of being. They are well aware of how their leader works and are used to it.

> We teachers work in teams where we can manage many issues. It quite often happens that Pascal comes to us with a whole host of questions and points of view. What he doesn't realise is that this is what we already do

FIGURE 10.1
The school's end-of-year Christmas celebration, December 2015. It was described as an emotional moment as Pascal had been gone for a while due to personal reasons and surprised everyone by coming in as Santa and Assistant Principal Petra Håkansson as Princess Leia. They had together successfully defeated Darth Vader. Photo: Jody Thompson, Still Vision Photography.

one teacher tells me and laughs. See Figure 10.1.

I chose to write a chapter about rule control versus trust-based control as I think that IES Sundsvall is often misunderstood. Yes a calm and secure work environment is something they deliver but they don't build it primarily on rules, control and punishment. When I have told different people that I am writing about Pascal and his leadership at the school, sometimes I have met this statement: "Oh, where it's so strict and authoritarian". My understanding is that this conclusion is easy to draw as a quick generalisation of the school. I think, just like the previous student Kim tells it, that it isn't the rules and control that made him change as a person. He changed when he got to learn that relationships are built on trust and when he got to experience that someone believed in him.

When Kim recently participated in thanking teachers who were leaving, he stood there together with the teenager who had thrown the first meatball. They both got to tell what the school meant for them. They had each received a T-shirt from Pascal to wear that day, On one, it said: "I threw the first meatball" and on Kim's it said: "Does anyone smell shrimp?" The story about the shrimp is something you will hear about soon but the conclusion of this chapter is that in a school, there needs to be structure, framework and control in order to build safety but these qualities alone are not enough. They are just the foundation to then having the potential to build relationships and build trust.

Kim can finish this chapter.

When I came to the school, it was in a period in my life when I was very unsure. I wanted to be tough and did many things at the school. One of the things I did was I put shrimps in the ventilation. Oh, how it stank! They had to sanitise the whole school. But the school helped me, the people who work there believe in the students that no one else believes in. I gave them zero respect, threw shit (not literally) and was angry, they did everything to understand why. When I began to break against my friendship circle, things started to change for me and the school awarded me with the prize "Biggest change". It gave me the motivation to continue on the right road. Mr. Brisson said: "There is going to be something good out of you!".

NOTES

1. Cockerell, L. (2008). *Creating Magic: 10 Common Sense Leadership Strategies from a Life at Disney*. New York: Doubleday Publishing Group.
2. Öppna jämförelser, SKL: "I Öppna jämförelser kan du jämföra information om kvalitet, resultat och kostnader inom vissa verksamhetsområden som kommuner, landsting och regionen ansvarar för." https://skl.se/tjanster/merfranskl/oppna jamforelser.275.html (07 November 2017).
3. Dolan, S. L., Garcia, S. and Richley, B. (2006). *Managing by Values, A Corporate Guide to Living, Being Alive, and Making a Living in the 21st Century*. London: Palgrave Macmillan, Page 75.
4. Team Lead at Internationella Engelska Skolan Sundsvall is a group at the school that acts as advisors to the leadership team. The group has representatives from most areas of the organisation. The union also has a representative in the group.

11

Yet Another Reorganisation!

Values are the most fundamental element of our road to success in the life of business and the business of life.

Simon L. Dolan[1]

When something doesn't work, you often quickly decide that there needs to be a change. At the same time, it feels like our personal need for change increases in speed. Take something as practical as the need to constantly renovate, move furniture around and work on our home. The couch in the living room is a good example of how the life length of things in our home has shortened. There is a pressure to change nowadays that has been made possible by technological developments and our high standard of living. This pressure for change is experienced by us as individuals, in our families, in society and of course also in our organisations and companies. I don't know if you have experienced a reorganisation—a few, maybe? As business, organisations and government conditions change rapidly, this has also resulted in an upswing of organisational changes. This in turn has introduced the concept of change management, which is a structured way of moving from the current situation to the desired position in the future. The method to achieving change management is through making positive behavioural changes which one believes can be sustainable.

The word change has high status today. If you are inclined towards change, open to development, take to new things easily and so on, then you are pointing forward and at the right time. People who are more against change or also actively go against change are called reactionary and brake blocks. The question is which of these kinds of people benefit from reorganisation? Often reorganisation is not done with the purpose of making things better for employees but rather reorganisation is about achieving results such as efficiency or better management and leadership. At the same time as we in many ways embrace change, there are few things that can create as much conflict or upset as change. Just changing place in an office can take a lot of energy from the team, and perhaps the completely open and flexible office landscape is a way to effectivise away all the discussions that changing offices usually causes. There is an unusual tension between preservation and change. Asking ourselves if the grass is greener on the other side is not something we ask just once or twice in life. Should we stay the same or do something new? As a leader in an organisation, you need to have decided how you look at this balance. It is important from how you put strategies in place and the daily work. When you employ people, you need to know and communicate what is expected at the workplace from the perspective of preservation and change. See Figure 11.1.

"We change all the time while at the same time, we don't change at all. We are adding small parts the whole time but they all fit into who we are" explains Pascal.

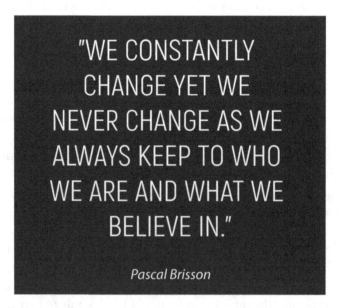

FIGURE 11.1
Pascal Brisson, Principal at Internationella Engelska Skolan describes how he sees change in the organisation he runs.

In some ways, Pascal has succeeded in different areas to get polar opposites to work together. It is precisely how I experience his leadership to be even in relation to standing still and changing. In spite of his drive, Pascal is surprisingly good at holding onto things. His colleague Jens agrees with Pascal's view of the organisation:

> We are very conservative here. Some things don't change and are there as a linchpin while other things change a lot. For example, we know exactly how a lesson should always start while our IT system School Soft is constantly changing without us even needing to think about it.

The school opened nine years ago and as I wrote earlier, it has been a quick journey from 250 students to now being over 1100 students. The question is if there has been during these nine years a need for a reorganisation to adapt to the new conditions when changing from a small to a big school.

> "We haven't done any big structural changes here at the school", says Pascal. "When we have grown, the structure hasn't actually changed but we have needed to strengthen different areas. For us it is about constantly refining how we do things, for example in what way we give feedback to our staff".

When you talk with Pascal's employees, you get the picture of a lot happening at the school.

"He wants to constantly evolve and you can be surprised that he has been here so long, he usually says: 'I'm building the boat, I'm not sailing it'" says Petra.

"How do teachers and other staff react to things happening all the time?"

"We have had a focus on how you can learn to accept change. The people we employ must be flexible and open to their job descriptions changing".

It is clear that not everything that happens is met with happiness and enthusiasm and this is something Pascal is aware of and says:

"Some complain about the changes, We are a school where we are very busy and work hard the whole time. But I think stagnation is worse than change".

> Change can also lead to insecurity in the face of something new, at the same time as the school is complex in nature and is work intensive. How do you support other leaders so they can feel secure in all this?

Again, we focus on what we want to achieve and it will be clear for the leaders what I expect of them. Leading up to 2018, a lot changed at the school and we began, two years ago to think about our roles. We are never done and when we notice that something doesn't work, we change it quickly. It is about testing and then doing when needed.

"When you change work tasks, do you usually get reactions?"

"Yes, sometimes parents don't like it and then we can explain why".

In spite of a personality that quickly reacts evolves all the time, there is also a great will and drive to take everyone with him and this is something Ralph has previously seen in Pascal.

Pascal is unbelievably proud of his school and is never satisfied. He never sits down and relaxes, he works the whole time. He is also very careful to make sure everyone is involved in decisions. This is something you can see in all the communication and dialogue now when he has decided to add to the school yet another year level and begin from grade 3.

Why Pascal doesn't see the need for any big changes to the organisation is in my opinion because he has succeeded in building a learning organisation. By this I mean: "An organization that continuously learns from its experiences with the purpose of completing its tasks in a better way".[2] At Internationella Engelska Skolan Sundsvall, there is constant work going into change and one of the absolutely most important variables for succeeding with this is: "the presence of one or more true leaders who can legitimize MBV by demonstrating the will, commitment and capability to deploy all the necessary resources".[3] He is, as I have described earlier in the chapter, a transformational leader. The similarity between his daily work with change and in leading big organisational changes is that all changes build some kind of worry and fear in people. To lessen this worry, communication is key. Following are some things to think about:[4]

1. Try to balance the change with information about things that will not change.
2. Communicate precisely what is expected of each person involved.
3. Communicate any specific difficulties foreseen so that nasty surprises are avoided.
4. Try to eliminate or reduce irrational fears (correct any misinformation circulating within the organisation).

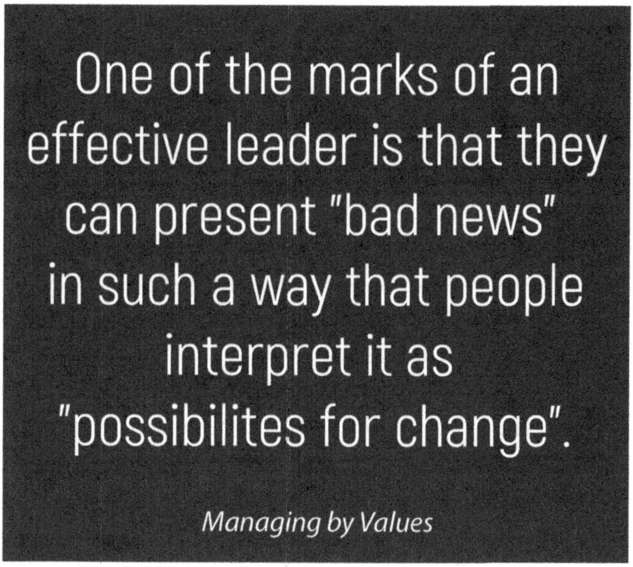

> One of the marks of an effective leader is that they can present "bad news" in such a way that people interpret it as "possibilites for change".
>
> *Managing by Values*

FIGURE 11.2
In the book *Managing by Values*, a quality that defines an effective leader is described.

5. Generate confidence in the intentions of the leaders.
6. Demonstrate that the first steps of the process, at least, are feasible.

Communication isn't something you do once to implement new key values or to inform about what is going to happen next week. Awareness of the importance of communication and knowledge of the work is crucial for a leader who wants others to follow. See Figure 11.2.

If you want to implement values-driven management through Management by Values (MBV) in your organisation, it isn't an organisational change that is needed but a change in the culture. How many times have you worked with changing the culture at your workplaces? I think that what actually is needed many times when organisations run on the spot or go in the wrong direction, is to change the culture. Not with the purpose of changing employees' behaviour and attitude but because you don't presumably have an organisation where beliefs, values, visions, goals and behaviour agree with each other. Here I am not going to go any deeper into tools and methods for implementing a successful and sustainable cultural change as that would be very extensive but I thought I would bring up some of the best ones I found from Dolan's and others' fantastic work.

In a process where culture must change, there needs to be people who are capable of managing complexity from five different roles.[5] There is a need for a *driver* that can be a person or a team. The driver sees the need for change, argues for it, advocates for change, mobilises emotions and reasons for change. The person or team must also have the position and power to be able to implement change. There needs to be a *sponsor* that usually carries the final responsibility for the success or failure of the change. The sponsor applies his or her legitimate power and authority to endow the change with political legitimacy to allocate the resources necessary for change. *Agents*, often several people, are those who execute, implement and put into practice the many technical aspects of the change. They see to it that the system or infrastructure needed is in place in terms of technology, education, focus groups or other elements to make sure the change is in agreement with the organisation's vision. The *facilitator* is more of a thinker than the agent. The facilitator provides advice, methodical and methodological reflection, and intervenes in the communications process in effecting change. The goal is to make sure that it is as friction-free a change process as possible and at the same time give advice to leadership about which changes should happen or not. The organisation's human resources staff are often connected to this role. The fifth role is the customer, the ones on the receiving end of the change. In principle, this is everyone in the organisation, more or less. The customer needs to be able to see for her/himself why the change is necessary and also participate in the design, implementation and monitoring of the change process.

The makers behind MBV describe something I often hear from people today, that is a frustration and tiredness at yet another change project. A frustration at yet another project that means adjustments to the organisation's image or other technicalities. I usually laugh a little at all the times my husband has come home and said it is time for yet another reorganisation. The workplace has changed name in his department so many times I can no longer keep track of exactly where he works. The workplace has been the same, except for a few room changes, and he has in principle had the same responsibilities and tasks. It is mostly just the name of the organisation and the personal titles that have changed. We humans seem to quite simply like change. It can be nice to rename things, but I think that in the long run, if this is the only visible result of the change process, then you're going to get tired of it pretty soon. The worst part is that soon it is no longer noticed. Dolan believes that many leaders in companies and organisations don't see their role in enabling change. When change processes fail, it is usually because there is no leader standing on the front line leading and legitimising real and desired changes such as beliefs and values. To succeed in making proper change in an organisation, and especially so if it is a little bigger, it is not enough to have only a change leader. It also needs a team that is specifically appointed to work on implementing the change, and not just taking the usual team as the risk is that they are not the right people for it or that their workload would then be too much. They would have to do what they normally do and at the same time, lead a big task implementing change. Most management systems are constructed from a situation of stability and not change and it is important to see that a time of change surely needs another management system. To really succeed with the transition from the present to the future organisation, specific structure and resources are needed. The most important aspect is that members in the change team are really convinced of the need for change and believe in the new concept. The team must drive the development towards change and at the same time, guide and have control over the whole process.[6]

There are three ways to implement a change according to the book *Managing by Values*. You can choose to do things yourself within the organisation. This means that management in the company tries to implement the change. This often results in tired leaders and has quite a bad effect out in the organisation. To get things to happen is another way. Here, the focus is on seeing that something happens. Then it isn't so important who does it or how it is done. If you choose this way to implement change, the leadership will need to ensure that those employed do what is needed. Then clear instructions or carrots and sticks are needed to get the right things to happen. The third choice that is in line with MBV is about making it possible for things to happen. The idea with this option involves all employees in the organisation in the work for change where the leader is the facilitator.[7]

If you are leading or managing a change process in an organisation, you are also going to automatically need to manage resistance to change. Each change requires effort to adapt to the new and this process tends to put people on the defensive. Dolan believes that if you don't get any resistance, then there was surely no need to implement a change.[8]

Change is for us humans something that is contradictory. We work differently in how much we strive for change and how much we appreciate it but it is a natural part of everyone's lives. When everything happens so quickly because we have driven it there, the balance between what should be kept and what should change becomes more important. I wanted with this chapter mostly to shine a light on and raise awareness of this. Personally, I think that we need more leaders that have the courage to take up cultural change instead of staying within the organisational structures. The organisation should constantly be adapting to the needs we have as a natural part of the organisation's development and it should not require a big change process. When the culture journey is complete and values management is implemented, the organisation becomes a learning organisation. That is where the change work is a part of the day-to-day with clear anchors in why we are there and what we believe in.

Dolan believes that we too often see change as something destructive that puts even more expectations on us when we already have too heavy workloads. This is not what he means with cultural change. He sees change as a powerful source for learning. Learning means that we first retest old ideas and then put new ideas into use. His tip is to ask ourselves how often we need to learn instead of asking how often we need to change; then the answer for most is—always.[9] Let us continue to learn together, it is one of my purposes with this book. I hope that this chapter can give you inspiration to continue learning. That is how we become change leaders and can build sustainable organisations. To end this chapter, here are some words from my new friend Simon who has taught me so much this year: "Organisations which will survive in the 21st century will have their employees capable of constantly 'de-learning' and 're-learning'; MBV provides a culture for reinforcing these capabilities".[10]

NOTES

1. Dolan, S. L. (2011). *Coaching by Values*. iUniverse, Page 4.
2. Nationalencyklopedin. Lärande organisation. http://www.ne.se/uppslagsverk/encyklopedi/lång/lärande-organisation (hämtad 28 July 2017).
3. Dolan, S. L., Garcia, S. and Richley, B. (2006). *Managing by Values, A Corporate Guide to Living, Being Alive, and Making a Living in the 21st Century*. London: Palgrave Macmillan, Page 149.
4. Dolan, S. L., Garcia, S. and Richley, B. (2006). *Managing by Values, A Corporate Guide to Living, Being Alive, and Making a Living in the 21st Century*. London: Palgrave Macmillan, Page 141.

5. Dolan, S. L., Garcia, S. and Richley, B. (2006). *Managing by Values, A Corporate Guide to Living, Being Alive, and Making a Living in the 21st Century.* London: Palgrave Macmillan, Pages 116–119.
6. Ibid., Pages 151–152.
7. Ibid., Pages 130–131.
8. Ibid., Page 133.
9. Ibid., Page 66.
10. Ibid., Page 115.

12

Motivation and Sustainable Drives

The best way to avoid the seven deadly flaws of extrinsic motivators is to avoid them altogether or to downplay them significantly and instead emphasize the elements of deeper motivation—autonomy, mastery, and purpose.

Daniel H. Pink[1]

We're sitting in Pascal's office and suddenly I hear feet stamping in time to music.

"Where is the music coming from, do you have a school dance or something?" I ask and laugh.

"Yes, absolutely, it's Friday music!"

"What do you mean?"

"Every Friday afternoon, we play music in the corridors".

Have you ever wondered about what motivates you to do different things? What is it that triggers you? In the role as teacher and parent, the word motivation has interested me a lot. To not just get things to happen for a moment but to build interest that continues over time. To successfully tap into every person's inner drive makes them want to try and do their best. Even if we are all different and have different things that drive us, I think that we humans are quite similar at our core and can function in similar ways. I am not competitive and it doesn't bother me to come last in a game. This has meant that as a teacher, I have had difficulty using forms of competition to motivate students to perform in the classroom. However, I love to use games and see this as on of man's very natural learning methods; children learn almost everything through play. At the same time, I have experienced it as a failing that I haven't really been able to meet those students who need competition to motivate them. I have had the same fight with myself when it comes to raising my children. When I had small children, there was a method of putting posters on the wall where children would get stars if they had done something good and the possibility of losing stars if they did something not so good. When the children didn't pick up after themselves or didn't want to clean, I thought maybe I should use some kind of reward system. Quickly, I saw that this wasn't for me as I wouldn't be able to deliver such a system in a credible way as I didn't really believe in it. I love to give praise, appreciation, feedback and rewards but not in some system of counting things out. In your leadership, knowledge about motivation can create an opportunity to get things to happen and to create a positive work environment. In this chapter, let us together discuss the concept of motivation and see its connection to values.

The embryo for this book was formed from different experiences over time. I explained in the introduction about a lecture that Pascal had many years ago that was about the work with values at Internationella Engelska Skolan Sundsvall (IESS). At the lecture, he gave recommendations of several books that he thought we should read. One of these books was *Drive* by Daniel H. Pink. I bought it and finally got to read a book that went into depth on what drives us as people and builds behaviour over time. The book became more interesting as it was recommended by Pascal who I thought represented a school where a lot was built on the so-called carrot and stick approach. Pink writes about, amongst other things, reward systems where the conditions are explained in advance to include performance connected to a prize—if you do this, you will get some candy or a job-related bonus. He believes that within this framework, you will succeed in getting the job done but you will not get creativity.[2] The reward system can be successful from a more long-term perspective if the reward comes as a surprise when one has done the job. Instead of saying: "If you do this" instead say: "Now that you have done this". What Pink means is that by giving rewards as surprises afterwards, the risk is less that you will see the reward as the reason for doing the task. If your job or tasks are motivated and driven by getting something instead of seeing the importance of the actual task, the risk is that the inner drive will be damaged. The book gives tools to build long-term sustainable drive and counteract the way we have taught ourselves to be people driven by short-term and quick incentives. We must protect our inner ability to motivate ourselves. Just as Internationella Engelska Skolan (IES) can easily be perceived as being successful because of strict rules, it is easy to believe that it is short-term reward systems such as trophies that motivate their students at school. What motivates managers, employees and students at the school, in my view, fits in well with what Pin writes: "The more the praise is about effort and strategy rather than about achieving a particular outcome—the more effective it can be".[3]

Organisations and workplaces often talk about it being more and more difficult to motivate employees. Even here it seems complexity has increased. Many talk about the younger generations growing up with "like buttons" in social media and that they need the same quick regular positive reactions in the workplace. At the same time, the need for the meaningfulness of being part of something bigger is increasing. To feel happiness, success and joy are strong driving forces and the will to earn a lot of money with little work is tempting. How will the future's workplaces look? What is going to motivate and drive the future workforce? What kind of leadership will that need? Here, schools are an important source of information about what is going to happen. The methods that are successful in schools today are most likely going to be successful in attracting, motivating and keeping future employees.

If you want an organisation where you go from control management to a culture of evolution, then you need to work on strengthening the motivation of employees. Dolan, Garcia and Richley, in their book *Managing by Values*[4] suggest that motivation in a company is of course crucial for its success but that motivation is not just based on traditional incentives from management level such as salary and tasks, but perhaps a few psychological factors and rewards as well.[5] They describe a number of what they see as the most important and motivating features of a workplace when it comes to psychological motivation.

1. **Autonomy**. Auto organisation of work processes, breaks and work habits.
2. **Variation**. The possibility to have variety in performing work.
3. **Identity**. The perception of owning the work processes and outcomes.
4. **Importance**. The belief that work outcomes are useful for oneself and the lives of others.
5. **Equity**. The perception of justice and fair play.
6. **Feedback**. Symmetry (both positive and negative) and coherence in getting feedback.

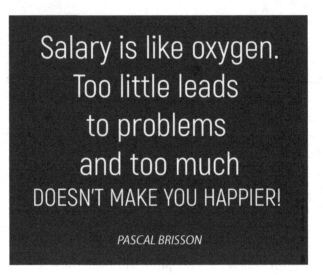

FIGURE 12.1
Principal Pascal Brisson on his view of salary as a tool for leaders to motivate their staff.

7. **Social support**. The belief that support will be given by colleagues, superiors and others when things get rough. See Figure 12.1.

What we need to think about is that the more psychological methods for building motivation don't work if there isn't a secure ground level of motivation, as Daniel H. Pink describes it: "The starting point, of course, is to ensure that the baseline rewards—wages, salaries, benefits, and so on—are adequate and fair".[6] Something that both Pink and Dolan describe in their different books is how you build motivation on a deeper level after seeing to some basic conditions: "MBV seeks to not only provide financial reward but aims to achieve high performance in day to day work by making it more meaningful".[7] What then has Pascal, as a leader, said about motivation from his perspective? He didn't bring up salaries himself in our discussions about motivation so I chose to ask him directly how he uses salaries as an instrument to recruit good people and motivate then when they are there?

> Salary is like oxygen. Too little leads to problems and too much doesn't make you happier. You need to find a fair level. It isn't that productivity increases automatically through higher salaries. At the same time, if salaries are too low, the focus is always on wanting a higher salary instead of the tasks you are supposed to be performing. What is most important when it comes to salaries is that it feels fair.

The answer from Pascal went on to be quite comprehensive, so I have chosen to make a list of his main points with some of my own extra comments.

1. **You need to know what you stand for and what you are to deliver.** We have through this book seen how this is clear at IES and in Pascal's leadership. This clarity makes something in the management by values (MBV) methodology possible, that is, that synergy is created where the organisation's values are harmonised with the values of the individual employee. When values are in tune, it becomes a great strength and provides stable ground for the motivation to go to work and perform your tasks. This synergy of values also provides the conditions in which employees know how to do their work.

2. **The feeling that you are a part of something bigger and that you are able to contribute to it.** This is about that the need for an organisation's vision and mission to be clear and relevant for all employees. The communication about the vision and mission should be done in such a way that everyone in the organisation feels that they see their part in the vision. We all need to understand the importance and meaning of our efforts. Here, the leader's story of the organisation and discussion with employees become the tools.

3. **You need to lift everyone up.** Pascal describes how he tries to lift everyone in their different situations and tasks, whether it is as a cleaner or an outgoing student. His ability to lift everyone was also something that the assistant principal, Petra talked about. "He is good at lifting people's strengths, and we get to be where we also have our strengths".

4. **Everyone needs to feel that they are developing as a person.** We have previously discussed man's need for and fear of change. The need to change is one of the driving forces behind us wanting to improve. We don't want to stand still in our own developmental curve. This doesn't need to mean that you change job description or title but can just as well be that you do it a little better or in another way. The school provides good opportunities for professional development but always with the starting point that it is relevant for the school and the person in question. Through getting feedback on this, you also build a feeling of receiving the opportunity to develop. Teachers at the school express that there is a big difference from other workplaces when it comes to the feedback you get. The school also

puts resources into people who have the job of supporting teachers to constantly improve their teaching and to maintain a good working environment in the classroom. Jens, a teacher, tells how the support team feel when they have a meeting with a student that has challenges in some way. This is what they do to help students develop:

> We want to focus on the positive. There is always a strategy when we meet a student. At the end of the meeting, we always focus on the positive and that the student now has the opportunity to make better choices. The organisation as a whole is characterised strongly by development and this is surely a result of wanting to also work on this at an individual level.

5. **It is important to have high expectations**. This has its basis in the philosophy of Internationella Engelska Skolan. There are high expectations from the founder Barbara on how to look at the parents' role. One of IES's cornerstones is to have high academic expectations. This goes for everyone, since their belief is that each child should be able to succeed no matter what their social background. For this to work, it needs to characterise the entire organisation, that is why there are high expectations on managers and principals. If a principal doesn't do their job, they don't get to stay. In the same way, principals have high expectations of teachers and other staff. The teachers are in an environment where it becomes very natural to also have high expectations of students.

6. **Success itself is motivating**. Pascal says: "Something we are good at is talking about our success, I think that success creates success. Sometimes we make the success something bigger than it really is", he says with a laugh. "Our success is important for us but also in communication with parents and students".

    The result of lifting people up and talking about success is that you create a feeling of pride within the organisation. You become a part of a winning team.

7. **Each person needs to feel seen for who they are**. This is about seeing each individual. This is something that Pascal feels they are really good at. It isn't so strange that it is so since it is a central point for the organisation. From the management team, there is a conscious effort to make sure everyone is seen. In practice, this is about seeing

people's strengths and weaknesses, discussing with each other what you burn for and want to work with, and at the same time, that managers have knowledge of the whole organisation to let you know what opportunities exist.

> During job interviews, I usually ask the person what their job would look like if they got to decide. I usually even ask, with a little smile, "What do you want to be when you grow up?"

To be seen and listened to creates a feeling of being a part of something. When Kim was a student at the school, he felt that the possibilities students had to participate in different ways strengthened solidarity and that meant that what the school had to teach had more impact.

With this chapter, I want to open up a bigger discussion about the question of motivation and what drives us to do what we do. With the right tools, it is possible to create motivation around the simplest or the most complex jobs. I think there needs to be a harmonisation when it comes to tools, the organisation's culture and values. To build motivation according to MBV's seven points, as described earlier in this chapter, the company must, for example, stand for fair and just game rules on all levels. The company leaders need to follow laws and to speak the truth to their employees. Even if Pascal, at that time, had never read anything about the MBV method for leading and managing an organisation, you can see that what he and the school does to build motivation is in agreement with this method. See Figure 12.2.

When I chose Pascal's leadership as an example for this book, it was partly because of his clear connection to values but also because his organisation showed really good results. The statistics show that Internationella Engelska Skolan Sundsvall is successful in creating a feeling of security and satisfaction in parents, students and staff. These are three very different groups and it would be interesting to hear how Pascal thinks he and his staff have succeeded in this.

> In short, it is about one: understanding what the specific group priori-tises first and two: to communicate that to the group. When for example it comes to parents, they want to come home and feel that they are good par-ents, they get that feeling if a happy child comes home who has also felt safe during the day. Students are a little bit more difficult to satisfy, there are so

FIGURE 12.2
Karin Henriksson and Petra Håkansson test the new swings in the staffroom at Internationella Engelska Skolan Sundsvall. Photo: Jody Thompson, Still Vision Photography.

many social aspects that come into play. We can have a good school from an academic perspective but it isn't enough to satisfy students. It is like a car that gets you from point A to point B but for most students, this is not enough. Students want to feel safe, to be themselves and to have good relationships with teachers. A difficulty with students is that what they want isn't always what they need, so satisfying them isn't always right. White fish for example, if we took that out of the menu at school, that would make the students happier.

Pascal compares this to how things are in schools in Canada. There, he reflects, you hardly ever assess what students and parents want and he sees a risk in how we do it in Sweden:

When we take in too much consideration what students and parents want, they become more like customers that we are trying to make happy instead of making sure we deliver what children and youths need. But in the system we have, it is important to get students to understand why. So for example, to get them to understand that when the school is clean, you feel good.

We have talked a lot about what you do to motivate your employees but how would you explain shortly what it is that makes your staff at the school give you high scores when it comes to questions about satisfaction and security?

It is difficult to say exactly what a teacher values most, even this is complex. They highly value getting feedback and that things are fixed quickly. I think that employees want to work here partly because we grow and evolve and because they feel that we have a good workplace with good facilities. It is a work environment where we challenge each other through both tough expectations and support. We are good at creating a feeling of community. This feeling is created through us being good at talking about the whole and giving a larger picture of what we do. Many value the combination of our social network and that we see the individual. We are interested in both what you as an individual want to do and what you experience as stressful. We have succeeded in recruiting many driven people and have the ability to place them where they have the opportunity to be successful.

One of the school's three main principles is a safe school environment. This principle makes it possible to create conditions for motivation in staff and students. According to MBV, the leader's role in a learning organisation is to create security:

One essential function of leaders and senior managers is to offer reassurance and emotional support. Anxiety derived from ambiguity or excessive insecurity blocks learning. In many companies, one of the main complaints of employees is the 'lack of support' from their bosses, who themselves probably feel they have enough to do to contain their own anxieties.[8]

Leaders must, especially during a period of change, be able to manage and lead themselves. Being a leader takes a lot of energy and even more when you are taking your organisation through a big change. It is necessary that the leader who is responsible for the process succeeds in controlling their own worry and being emotionally balanced, not just to be able to take care of conflicts or challenges along the way.[9] Pascal has during his years as principal found himself in a continual process of change when he has continually chosen to see the school grow. He has quite a large turnover of staff when it comes to those who come from other countries as they are often there a couple of years and then want to go back to their homeland. On top of this, every school year has meant new employees since the organisation has grown. In the middle of this, he is a person who is driven in part by worry and anxiety. Here, I have asked myself how the school can get such high results when it comes to feeling secure. I therefore asked Pascal how he worked with feeling safe.

> Feeling safe is about many different things but it is one of the cornerstones of our school. If students don't feel safe, they can't concentrate. Initially, it is about analysing which areas and where security is most important. Is it outside, in the corridors or other places? We also ask when and in which situations students feel insecure. When we know the answer to where and when, we can discuss how we build security. Then it can be about routines or our 'Classroom 10 must haves'. The next level is about 'tough love', that is consequences and support. It is about the small details each day like me going around the school between 11am and 1pm and that we always react quickly when something happens. We know what we are going to do and how important it is. When we grow, we need to refine our routines and we have always had routines for 'lock down', that is when we quickly need to lock the school down in the middle of activities. More and more, we engage ourselves in what is happening outside the school and in the digital world. Some parents have a little too high expectations of the school but we show self assurance in that we can help but at the same time tell parents what they are responsible for. We need parents' support and they need to feel that they can trust that the school will do what we say we will.

"This is a lot about how you ensure this safe working environment. How can you as a leader also support your staff to not feel anxiety or worry?"

> Here I have a lot of help from Pieter with how we work together with teachers. It is partially about them feeling secure in what we expect of them, that we are consistent in our behaviour, that we give support and at the same time react quickly. We value togetherness, have fun together, it should feel natural to joke with the principal, and we listen and give information. It is the complex connection between different things that mean that they feel safe. It is very important how we communicate. Take this 'lock down' where we have had to lock the whole school and students have been locked in the classrooms and followed our security routines. Of course, children are affected by this. Through how we communicate, we want the situation to feel both safe and at the same time we teach them that the world isn't safe.

To go back to motivation, it is an organisation's intention to in some way create an environment that results in long-term and sustainable commitment from employees to do the work they must do. If a company really wants to improve how employees perform, company leaders need to constantly improve the system for wage allocation, bonuses, working hours, opportunities to improve, career options and other ways to give meaningful rewards. This is as important as it is to at the same time redesign the psychosocial working conditions such as independence, job tasks, feedback, the importance of what you do, fairness and support. To also succeed in motivating staff to be true to the company's values, efforts to do so should be rewarded, be they through economic rewards or through other ways. One of the greatest problems from an employee perspective is if there is a mutual understanding that one's efforts are not noticed.[10] In Pascal's lecture, he talked about what he and his employees do to show the importance of the school's values daily. One example he talked about was that those at the school are careful to keep it clean and looking good. If you see rubbish on the floor, it is expected that you pick it up. He told how he, at one point, walked the corridors and saw a teacher bend down and pick up a little piece of paper. The first thing he wanted to say with the story is that it shows that the teachers at the school act. The next aspect he wanted to communicate was what response this teacher had who didn't know that the principal was watching. Pascal said that he caught up with the teacher to praise them and here he emphasised the importance of what you say. It isn't enough to just say "Well done!", in a values- and culture-promoting job; good communication is central. "Hi, I saw that" he said. Then you should confirm that you understood exactly what was done: "you picked up a paper from the floor and threw it in the bin" and then, last but most importantly, connect it to the values: "that is exactly what we do here at the school where we have a safe and orderly school environment". Here you strengthen mutual values and it becomes a fantastic starting point for motivating and at the same time you reward the right behaviour and create more motivation and from there strengthen the organisation's culture and connection to their own beliefs.

Finally, I want to add something I read on the website for Internationella Engelska Skolan Sundsvall on the page where the principal has the floor. This quote shows the power of communication to paint a picture of who you are as an organisation. The picture can be decisive for motivation: "Through this website you will get an opportunity to go backstage at one of Sundsvall's most vibrant and unique workplaces. /Pascal Brisson".[11]

NOTES

1. Pink, D. H. (2009). *Drive*. Riverhead books, Page 62.
2. Pink, D. H. (2009). *Drive*. Riverhead books, Page 64.
3. Pink, D. H. (2009). *Drive*. Riverhead books, Page 66.
4. Dolan, S. L., Garcia, S. and Richley, B. (2006). *Managing by Values, A Corporate Guide to Living, Being Alive, and Making a Living in the 21st Century*. London: Palgrave Macmillan.
5. Ibid., Page 111.
6. Pink, D. H. (2009). *Drive*. Riverhead books, Page 58.
7. Dolan, S. L., Garcia, S. and Richley, B. (2006). *Managing by Values, A Corporate Guide to Living, Being Alive, and Making a Living in the 21st Century*. London: Palgrave Macmillan, Page 22.
8. Dolan, S. L., Garcia, S. and Richley, B. (2006). *Managing by Values, A Corporate Guide to Living, Being Alive, and Making a Living in the 21st Century*. London: Palgrave Macmillan, Page 108.
9. Ibid., Page 131.
10. Ibid., Page 193.
11. Internationella Engelska Skolan Sundsvall. Welcome from the Principal. https://sundsvall.engelska.se/sv/about-our-school/welcome-principal (15 June 2017).

13

Stress and Belonging!

A new type of toxic agent comes to bear. One which has no color and no odor but causes suffering, illness and sometimes even death.[1]

S. Dolan, S. Garcia, B. Richley

The question that Simon L. Dolan asked himself in the 1970s about work-related stress's effect on our health is extremely relevant today. The consequences of stress are one of the biggest health issues of our time. Stress makes us physically and psychologically sick and can in its most extreme form be fatal. When Dolan started to study the connection between work-related stress and heart attacks, it started his journey towards formulating a new way to manage and lead organisations. To manage through values, and according to the method Management by Values (MBV) provides, organisations can take the focus away from constantly striving after results and efficiency, which easily evokes stress, and instead focus on a management style that lowers stress-related illness. Perhaps we don't see as Dolan did that heart attacks are the clearest consequences, but stress affects our bodies in different ways mentally, emotionally and physically, any of which can put a stop to and hinder our ability to work. The body is drained in such a way that it causes huge consequences for that particular person, those closest to them, for their workplace and even for society as a whole. This is how Aleksander Perski, associate professor at Stockholm University's stress study institute puts it: "The people with the most sick leave work in schools, health and social care and are often middle-aged women. That is the biggest risk group for stress related illness right now".[2] In the municipal organisation in my municipality, the number of people on sick leave is increasing and it has been like that for many years. It is greatest in health and social care and schools but we are also seeing an increase in other areas that are more administrative. Interventions are done, resources are allocated and everyone is worried but it still seems to be difficult to get a large ship to change course. We can blame societal trends as a whole and we see overall in Sweden an increase in the level of psychological ill-health, especially in middle-aged women. Today we vaccinate our children against illnesses that previously were fatal but we haven't succeeded in hindering more and more children from showing symptoms of stress. We need to have the courage to leave no stone unturned to counteract this development. This book doesn't present a solution but I am convinced that leadership has a huge importance in improving health. It is about your own leadership over yourself, parents' leadership, leadership in both private and public sectors as well as political leadership from the municipality to the world's community. At the base, it is about values and how we value ourselves, others and everything around us.

It is actually perhaps wrong to give this question its own chapter. I actually think the whole book has tools for creating a more sustainable lifestyle and work life. There is no business management system worth its salt that sees it as beneficial for employees to be unwell no matter whether the driving force is of economic or human character. We all want the same thing, that people are well. Internationella Engelska Skolan Sundsvall (IESS) has, just like many other school and workplaces, stress-related problems while at the same time, many there express happiness and pride at being able to work there. The school is practicing Management by Values, as the management acts from beliefs, values and principles; however, at the same time, high expectations and goals are expected from you. In the school survey from Skolinspektion from Autumn 2016, where pedagogical staff were surveyed, there were some areas that showed another type of leadership at IESS compared to other schools. When it came to pedagogical leadership of the principal, high points were awarded from pedagogical staff. When it came to the principal's knowledge about daily work, how the principal promotes student development as well as how the principal takes responsibility for the pedagogical work, the school had results of 9.8, 9.7 and 9.7 out of 10, respectively. The total index for pedagogical leadership at Internationella Engelska Skolan (IES) in Sundsvall was scored 9.7 compared with the average of all the other schools that participated in the survey who had an index of 7.4. Another area that relates a lot to the principal's role at the school is the development of education. Here the questions were about how the principal uses student surveys to improve education, how the principal takes part in and changes the ways students work if they are not passing as well as if the principal listens to the pedagogical staff and sees that it leads to relevant changes in how they work. If we look at the results from this area's total index, IESS was scored 9.5, compared with other schools who had an average result of 6.9. From this statistic, it is possible to draw the conclusion that the school has very present leadership. This in turn means that employees have support in their work, which of course leads to a better working environment. That is why there is a chapter about how Internationella Engelska Skolan Sundsvall manages and works to prevent stress. Not because they are without stress but to learn how they think and work with a challenge that society has today, especially in our school environments.

We see work-related stress and ill-health not just in teachers but even in school leaders and principals. In leadership positions, we generally see a large staff turnover and the risk of stress is high. This is why I wanted to start by asking how, within his role as principal, he feels.

"How are you feeling Pascal?"

A good question that is not so simple to answer. I have worked as principal of a school for ten years which shows that I in some way have made it work during a quite long period of time. There is a lot of stress and sometimes it is overwhelming. To be responsible for others' behaviour can lead to stress. It is quite easy to be responsible for your own behaviour but when you suddenly need to be responsible for other people's behaviour, the stress increases.

"Being a principal is an exposed position and just as you Pascal describe it, there is a lot of responsibility in the role. How do you work as a person when it comes to stress?

My personality is such that I am not calm by nature. This is a weakness of mine which can harm both me and those around me. I am very aware of this and try to think about it. For example, I surround myself with people who are calm and have another form of energy. This is a way to help myself manage everything that happens. To lead a school is extremely complex. We have direct contact with thousands of people who have a direct interest in how the school is managed. On top of this, we manage the most important thing in their lives—their children. This means that their behaviour isn't always rational and that can be very stressful.

"What do you think is the toughest to manage?

> The most difficult is when colleagues react to news they have been given or go from something being a certain way without them having all the information. Sometimes it is information that I can't share which makes it very difficult for me to explain the situation. These types of situations are both stressful for me and for my colleagues.

"How is IESS as a workplace from the perspective of stress and how do you as a leader manage it?"

> Our school works in a very intensive way. We push ourselves very hard. This means that this type of working environment does not suit everyone. Just like not everyone can work at Apple, not everyone can work at IESS. My job is to continue to put pressure on while at the same time as I make sure I don't push too much. Sometimes I make the mistake of pushing too hard. This affects me too, of course. But then I try, as soon as I can to see this and hold back a little. There is a line that we must always balance on. I see it as impossible to hold myself on one side of the line the whole time but we try to adapt as we go.

"So, if you would summarise how you feel as Principal Pascal Brisson?"

"It depends on the day and the week. Some days are simple while others are difficult. But my long-term motivation for what we build together is still strong and gives me energy".

At the beginning of the 20th century, the German-American psychologist Kurt Lewin had already laid the groundwork for the concept and method of organisation development (OD). Since then, OD has developed and is today, in contrast to the natural continual change that occurs in organisations, a defined change process. This organisational change focuses on increasing efficiency in organisations, both in the long and short term. This is done by improving processes and structures that support individuals, groups and systems development. The core of it is built on creating a learning environment where continual work for change is carried out by the whole organisation.[3] You are perhaps wondering what this has to do with stress and values management? There is a lot of research behind OD that coincides with MBV and contributes to sustainable improvements. OD in itself is based on a number of core values and is therefore clearly grounded in values as a starting point. One of these values is about having a genuine interest in the quality of life[4] or as in another definition I found: "to value the whole person".[5] The value is described further like this: "In order to help individuals maximize their potential in an organization, we respect that people are complex. Therefore, we work hard to understand individuals have diverse needs, skills, and feelings and respect those differences in our work with them".

To be able to manage the stress of others is a lot about seeing and understanding the whole person. As a leader, you need to know who you are working with and not just what the person has done or wants to do. This is relevant if you are going to lead already recruited staff or if you are recruiting new staff. You need to put energy, time and power into this to then be able to decide if the employee is in the right place in the organisation or perhaps even to decide that the person isn't in the right workplace. In discussions with Pascal, it comes up that when a person wants to see the whole individual, it means constant work that is never done. Situations change, people change and complex situations require a continual discussion about what must be kept and what must change. To see the person means listening to them and participating in the organisation. It is also about providing frameworks and rules that build security. And perhaps most importantly, to ensure they feel that something is happening as a result of being seen. When I talked to Pieter about stress and how they work with it, this was his first response:

"When someone brings up stress or we notice that someone doesn't feel good as they are feeling negative stress, something happens right away".

Teachers explain that they feel security in that they amongst the staff often check with each other on how they are feeling. If they feel stress or if something feels difficult, they get support and help.

> Of course there is stress at this workplace, we have high expectations of ourselves and others. At the same time, we who work here want it to be that way. The high expectation makes us feel satisfied with what we do

says teacher Jocelyn.

"I get more stressed in an environment where there is not structure. At other workplaces, I have felt another type of stress", explains Mattias. "Additionally, my picture is that we here at the school discover negative stress early and then you can find options for that person".

Jocelyn continues:

"Here, we talk openly about stress and there are routines on how we manage it".

"I think that this is an advantage that we are good at communication. Pascal is good at informing us. Not knowing, that is something that creates stress. At our APT (workplace meeting) we talk about both economy, security and communication", adds Jens to the discussion.

> We have thought a lot about how to take care of each other as we have many international teachers who don't have any family here. We must give more support than usual. Many of our staff have also said that this is their first workplace which also means we need to engage ourselves more with the staff. We try to act in time so everyone will feel good but of course we don't always succeed. When someone feels stressed, we see that we do what we can to help

says Pascal.

> The staff at your school say in surveys that they are happy, feel secure and feel that they have opportunity to grow. They seem to feel quite good despite the development in Sweden of an increase in the number of teachers on sick leave because of stress. What do you think you do differently?

> We are good at creating a structure and taking away tasks from teachers so that there is less for them to think about. That we know what is expected of us builds security and no one needs to be surprised and panic. We give support when something happens and that is something I want us to be even better at. We want to be able to build an even better structure for working with this. But I think the most important thing is to create clarity by explaining what we stand for and which routines are applicable

says Pascal.

"Pascal is there anything that makes you unable to sleep at night?"

"Yes, an organisation that doesn't work makes me stressed and then I can't sleep when Friday evening comes around".

I described earlier in the chapter how good relationships make performances of high quality possible within an organisation. Healthy, good and dynamic relationships are more difficult to achieve in an environment that is characterised by stress. Dolan and his co-writers believe that "Stress occurs at the individual level when his or her workload or responsibilities are perceived to be too great or heavy for the available mental and emotional resources".[6] For an individual to gather strength to manage their stress, they mean that what is needed is to find a balance between the time spent working, with family and for themself. For real business leaders, it is necessary to devote yourself to working conditions as well as the physical and psychological ones.

In the end, I think that there is a lot that has been described in this chapter of this book that works for employees and managers' health in an organisation. Basically, everyone needs encouragement and emotional support for good health, while it is in uncertainty and insecurity that ill-health and stress are fostered. You can wonder why these old truths are so difficult to live up to today. What actually hinders us from finding the answer? My contribution to our discussion in this book is that many methods we use to manage and lead, such as Management by Instructions or Objectives, hinder us from acting in a sustainable way. The right things must come first. I mean that it should be the values and not the results. But for this, courage from leaders is needed to have the energy to engage in humans and defend the time it takes. This doesn't guarantee total health but it creates an environment where every person feels good. You also feel good when you are seen and feel acknowledged by those around you acting from who you are and how you feel, no matter if it is a fantastic day or one of the toughest. The reactions Pascal got when he didn't write his individual Christmas letters to the staff, as I talked about in Chapter 10, show how much a personal connection matters. The event made him write a summer letter instead when he himself had gathered enough energy.

> To see the individual is very important. I learnt that if I stop doing something for my employees that usually makes them feel seen, it can affect them very negatively. This I have learnt the hard way at the same time as I got the opportunity to see how much my efforts actually mean

says Pascal.

Or is it perhaps as Pascal expressed it at the beginning of this chapter that it is the vision for the future that gives power? Here he and Dolan are in agreement: "Optimistic expectations are the fuel of change...The generation of an optimistic and positive feeling towards change depends in large measure on the creation and presentation of a clear and attractive vision of the future".[7] This means that a vision isn't just important to knowing the direction or to define the company, when correctly formulated and communicated, the vision is a source of energy, power and motivation.

There is a word in English, "aligned", and the word is used a lot by Dolan when he talks about MBV and I have come to like it very much. Especially to be able to understand why I as a leader or employee enjoy being in or don't like being in an organisation or not. It is simply that when the workplace's values are aligned with your own values, it feels right from many perspectives. From this, I want to end the chapter with a quote I found when I surfed around the net a little: "Everything that keeps you from being yourself causes stress".[8]

NOTES

1. Dolan, S. L., Salvador G. and Richley, B. (2006). *Managing by Values, A Corporate Guide to Living, Being Alive, and Making a Living in the 21st Century*. London: Palgrave Macmillan, Page 208.
2. Stridsman, S. Sjukskrivningar för stress ökar. Skolvärlden. http://skolvarlden.se/art iklar/sjukskrivningar-stress-okar (01 August 2017).
3. Dolan, S. L., Garcia, S. and Richley, B. (2006). *Managing by Values, A Corporate Guide to Living, Being Alive, and Making a Living in the 21st Century*. London: Palgrave Macmillan, Page 97.
4. Ibid., Page 99.
5. Ethics in Organizational Development. Organizational development core values. http://odethics.weebly.com/od-core-values.html (01 August 2017).
6. Dolan, S. L., Garcia, S. and Richley, B. (2006). *Managing by Values, A Corporate Guide to Living, Being Alive, and Making a Living in the 21st Century*. London: Palgrave Macmillan, Page 104.
7. Dolan, S. L., Garcia, S. and Richley, B. (2006). *Managing by Values, A Corporate Guide to Living, Being Alive, and Making a Living in the 21st Century*. London: Palgrave Macmillan, Page 142.
8. Citatburken. https://www.citatburken.se/s/allt-som-h%C3%A5ller-dig-borta-fr% C3%A5n-att-vara-sig-sj%C3%A4lv-orsakar-stress-116702/ (02 August). Translation Majorie Challis.

14

Steps to Make Management by Values (MBV) Happen

As proposed throughout this text, change for the sake of change has never been the philosophy of MBV.[1]

S. Dolan, S. Garcia, B. Richley

Now that we are towards the end of the book, I hope that you have a new or deepened knowledge about the management and leadership model Management by Values (MBV). My descriptions are not a complete summary of MBV; I have cherry-picked what I personally see as the first necessary step to a sustainable and successful leadership in our time. In this chapter, I explain steps you can take to implement MBV in an organisation. If you want, you can of course choose to take a few parts from this management and leadership model based on what suits you and your organisation. I really hope that you do it so you can test and see what will happen. If you want to implement MBV completely, it is a huge task of change on all levels, but it begins with values. I am going to describe the steps or different phases, that the authors of the book *Managing by Values*[2] consider to be fundamental to the process of introducing MBV. They divide the process into two main phases: The first phase is focused on getting the change you want to really happen, and the second phase is focused on ensuring that those changes you have chosen to aim for remain in the organisation. See Figure 14.1.

- **Phase 0**. This phase occurs before the change starts to take form. In this phase, a trustworthy leader must be found to implement change. Pascal was chosen to start a new school which involves a big creation

Step-by-step to put MBV into practice

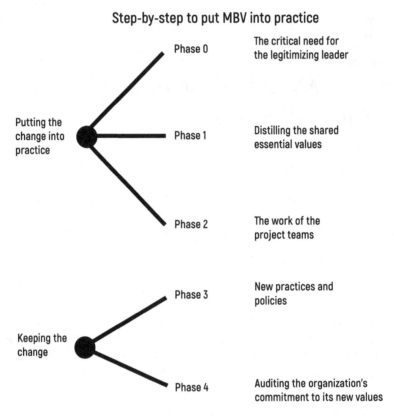

Phase 0 — The critical need for the legitimizing leader

Putting the change into practice

Phase 1 — Distilling the shared essential values

Phase 2 — The work of the project teams

Phase 3 — New practices and policies

Keeping the change

Phase 4 — Auditing the organization's commitment to its new values

FIGURE 14.1

The different phases for implementing MBV in an organisation. Ibid., Page 149. Used with permission from Simon L. Dolan. Figure created by Norlins förlag.

and change process. He in turn has chosen managers to be able to continue to take the school forward in a process of continuous change. The leader or leaders in this phase need to have the right personal energy, have the economic resources that are needed, and most importantly, they need to have the required amount of time.

- **Phase 1**. During this phase, the mutual fundamental values are crystallised. We discussed this in Chapter Eight, the chapter about vision, mission and the more operative values. In this phase, the strategic parts of the organisation are formulated. What is raised as central is participation and that a joint effort is required to secure engagement in the long term. First, you need to formulate a common image of what future you want that should be described and expressed as final values to then become a part of the vision and the mission. Second, you need participation in analysing the organisation's current set of values through a SWOT analysis to measure them up against the opportunities and threats of the organisation's environment. The SWOT is carried out on the level of values rather than by-and-large competencies. Ask what are our current values, and what are their weaknesses? How do our values stand in terms of threats and opportunities in this environment and in this society, that we find ourselves in? The third and final step has the task of making sure there is a consensus around where we are going to achieve change together. Here you need to formulate new instrumental values to reform the current organisational culture. In choosing instrumental values, you need to, according to MBV, have a starting point in the triaxial 3E-model and classifications of values, as were described earlier in this book.

A. **Economic-pragmatic values**: These are important for support functions to work in the organisation. Areas such as economy, planning and quality work are connected.

B. **Ethical-social values**: These values are for the group and affect how people behave. They guide how you behave in public, at work and in relationships with others. Some examples of these values are honesty, respect and loyalty.

C. **Emotional-developmental values**: These values are foundational for creating new opportunities for things to happen. They are connected to trust, freedom and happiness. Examples of these values are creativity, fulfilment and flexibility.

As always, when it comes to values, they need to be explained and put into use so they are not just pretty words. They need to be concrete and understandable to have any effect.

- **Phase 2**. Here cultural changes are translated into real changes in the workplace's attitudes, institutional processes and tasks. Now the talking is done and defined values are now the goal for changes. In this phase, it is recommended that you use different project teams, where each one has a specific mission and area of responsibility where the values are to be implemented.

- **Phase 3**. The work with internal policies and especially those that are connected to human resources is now taking place to ensure that the change you choose will be implemented and become the current organisational culture. This needs to be done in particular in three areas. The first is the use of values in recruitment, that is, when staff members are employed. As described earlier, it is difficult to force values onto a person or to try to convince someone to change their values. It is therefore necessary to look for people who already share the values. One condition to getting the right person for the job is that the organisation has values that are in line with the vision and mission. Then the person needs to have values in line with the organisation's culture, and the person's qualities and competencies for the job need to be right. The other thing that needs to be done to maintain the change you have chosen is to make sure that training, education and development happen according to an expressed strategy. Planned and continual education is key to implementing those values that are mutually decided; they are crucial to the organisation's success. The third part is to evaluate performance based on values and recognise efforts that are in line with the values. To encourage continuous development and improvement, both monumental and non-monumental rewards should be in place.

- **Phase 4**. All too often, we have seen examples of how someone has created a fancy strategy document for the organisation with new well-formulated vision, mission and instrumental values but after that, nothing more happens. The company's management need to take responsibility to continually evaluate and reward employee performance and behaviour from how they match the strategy:

> But beyond the successful adoption of a new culture, MBV also postulates the desirability of making that culture dynamic, with commitments by all employees to continuous learning, continuous improvement, periodical reviews of values, and the induction of new employees into the culture.[3]

This last phase is important for the MBV method as it isn't implemented until you know that the result is as intended. The authors believe that you can use the tool revision that we usually use that is connected to economy to from an MBV perspective assess that the behaviour and activities agree with the principles, legislation, guidelines and strategies formulated by the company's management. For this to work however, employees must see the value of the revision.

Of course, there are many challenges along the way and there is no simple model to help you go through a cultural change in an organisation or to be a dynamic and evolving organisation. In this book, I bring up important key ideas from MBV for the kind of leadership needed today and in the future. At the same time as there being some simple and old truths, the solutions are complex. Time, engagement and a lot of discussion are needed to use the method correctly in the situation you find yourself in, or as expressed in the book *Managing by Values*: "Managing by values is an investment in the present and future of your organization in the present and future of your organization but one that requires time and resources".[4] Perhaps the most important thing to take with you is that it isn't a project that takes one or two years, it takes longer than that. This means that you need a leader and employees that continually work with it. If you as a company manager or leader in the public sector want to deepen your understanding, I can recommend the book *Managing by Values*. If you are more interested in your own personal leadership or want to improve as a coach, the book *Coaching by Values* is very concrete in how you can both think and act. I want to round off this chapter with something from Dolan and his co-authors: "Also, if you think a culture change can ever be effectively 'finished' then you really don't understand what it is all about (Go back to the beginning of the book!)".[5]

NOTES

1. Dolan, S. L., Garcia, S. and Richley, B. (2006). *Managing by Values, A Corporate Guide to Living, Being Alive, and Making a Living in the 21st Century*. London: Palgrave Macmillan, Page 148.
2. Dolan, S. L., Garcia, S. and Richley, B. (2006). *Managing by Values, A Corporate Guide to Living, Being Alive, and Making a Living in the 21st Century*. London: Palgrave Macmillan, Page 148.
3. Ibid., Page 195.
4. Ibid., Page 104.
5. Ibid., Page 206.

15

Success Is Knowing What You Stand For!

Pascal is very considerate, thoughtful and brave. At the same time, he never hesitates to say what he is thinking.

Barbara Bergström

Karin Henriksson stood quite far down the corridor of the school. She stood together with a student who didn't want to go into the classroom. It was the morning before the first lesson would begin and the corridor was full of students. "Suddenly I see a hand stick up in the throng of students and everyone was suddenly silent. This is what IESS is for me" says Karin.

This book gives a picture of Internationella Engelska Skolan Sundsvall (IESS) from my point of view and the perspective of leading by values. Now, at the end of the book, I want to give space to Pascal and his employees to tell what they themselves feel characterises their organisation and what is the reason for their mutual success. Karin summarises it like this:

We walk together, we have the same rules and we say WE.

Success is a word that needs to be defined. How you look at the word success and how you see it has a strong link to your values. The word success is used in communication from Internationella Engelska Skolan. On the website for IESS, where you can read about the school, it says: "We look forward to many more years of success in Sundsvall!".[1] I asked Pascal what that meant in practice. "That we deliver what we promised, that is, our vision. That students continue to achieve good academic results and feel safe. That our staff continue to develop".

"What is it first and foremost that has made your leadership and success for this organisation possible?"

> Freedom and if I didn't succeed, I would not still be here! The nice thing is that I as a principal in IES can be very independent. I and we as a local school have a lot of power which makes it possible for us to make our own decisions. The success builds on there being a clear idea of what the school is to deliver which is grounded in some values. Then it is up to the principal to design his or her school, that is, how you do it is up to you.

"My picture is that out of the statistics that can be found, your school is one of the best in Sweden, I know that you don't really like to compare yourself to other schools in that way, but if I were to ask you like this: What is it that makes you a good school that succeeds academically and an organisation that seems to hold over time?"

> We have a clear understanding of who we are, what we want to build and we have the courage as well as the ability to constantly deliver while at the same time, we live with the paranoia about losing what we have built. We have advantages in many different ways. For example, I have been able to choose all the staff. I also think that the staff here can feel secure as I worry about everything

says Pascal and smiles. "A disadvantage is that we are a publicly funded independent school and we are therefore seen to be 'on the wrong side'. There are many who work against us because of this".

"What is your greatest lesson after your ten years as leader for an organisation under constant development and expansion?"

"The most important lesson has been to have a clear picture and know how you are going to implement it. We are successful as we quickly communicate what we believe, paint a picture and then deliver it". See Figure 15.1.

Another strength that Pascal emphasises in this context is that he not only has the opportunity to choose staff but the design of the whole process around the staff is important:

"We test how people fit with us and see how they can be a good complement. When the person is then there, we try to support them as much as we can and that is our biggest strength". You met one of the first recruits earlier in the book, Petra who is today assistant principal. I asked her what the reason for the school's success is:

> PASCAL BRISSON:
>
> "We succeed because we quickly communicate what we believe in, paint a clear picture and then deliver it."

FIGURE 15.1
Principal Pascal Brisson about what he thinks is necessary to achieve success at Internationella Engelska Skolan Sundsvall.

A lot is built on that the school has a good concept and when it was established in Sundsvall, there was a need for a good school. Our school would surely have succeeded without Pascal as principal but he has introduced Canada with his own background and that has placed a special characteristic on the organisation. Then I don't think that we would have been so big so quickly if it weren't for Pascal who is a 'builder'.

"What is the good concept you have?"

"We focus the whole time on our beliefs, and nothing in our main meetings or in any other situation is said randomly".

"Why do you like to work at the school?"

Because the staff agree that here we work from the idea of 'no child left behind' and 'tough love' and that is how we are towards each other and not just towards the students. For this to be possible, Pascal is very important. He must present a good example, otherwise no one else would follow.

"Are there other strengths in Pascal's leadership that affect your success?"

"He has never had a problem with asking for help and he is very quick to get things going. It is what he is good at and his best sides that irritate us most", says Petra and laughs. "He is very much focused on solving problems and fixing things very quickly, sometimes a little too quickly so he steps in and solves things before the rest of us have had a chance to do it".

"Communication seems to be a part of your school's strengths, in what way does he participate in this?"

> We believe in communication in everything we do and it is important for the whole organisation. Communication is something that Pascal encourages. Some days ago, I found an old photo in my phone from when we as a school participated in a parade. I sent it to Pascal to show him something fun that felt like something that was typically us. Instead of getting a laugh or happy comment, I got the reply: 'We have to get an Instagram account'. That is typically him, always with the new ideas and new things.

"What do you think characterises good leadership?"

> We aren't scared to move people around or make adjustments in the organisation. But if you are to be a good boss, you have to bond with your employees and involve as many as possible in the process before you make changes

Petra believes.

"Would Pascal as a leader work in other situations do you think?"

"Wherever he would be boss, he needs to be able to be who he is. His leadership qualities show the teacher in him. He cares about everyone, expects them to deliver, pushes and is quick to take care of things". See Figure 15.2.

In the group of teachers I have spoken with, they describe having the same leader over time as a strength. If we look back to Chapter Six about what it takes to be a leader, and Chapter Seven about how to create teammanship, we see how Pascal as a person has had a big influence on how the job should be done and on reaching the vision of the Internationella Engelska Skolan (IES). He has interpreted what the company's beliefs mean for the school. He has been involved in all the recruitment and active in communicating and supporting how others communicate. He has also had a strong influence on the culture at the workplace. Without exaggerating a leader's role, this book shows what great meaning an active and engaged leader has. It would surely have been a good school even if Pascal had been replaced in these ten years but it would probably have disrupted and changed operations in several central areas. Outside of whether the changes that would have been implemented would have been better or worse, a change takes energy and is difficult to implement; therefore, continual leadership is a strength.

FIGURE 15.2
Petra Håkansson shows a photo from when Internationella Engelska Skolan Sundsvall participated in a parade. It was this photo that made Pascal want to start an Instagram account for the school. Photo: Jody Thompson, Still Vision Photography.

VOICES ON THE LEADERSHIP'S IMPORTANCE FOR THE SCHOOL'S SUCCESS

There are of course many reasons for IESS' successes and I think that the leadership is one of them. I have chosen to ask different people about how they look at the connection between Pascal's leadership and the school's success. Anna-Maria says that him being available has been important.

> There is a strong interest in participating in the running of the school. Pascal's presence in the classroom and corridors is central. Our leaders are a part of the organisation and are interested in what happens. What others usually say about us is that we have a principal who stands in the school-yard every morning to welcome students.

In this book, I hope that you also have been able to read that it isn't a lone person that makes a difference, it is about building the team. Nevertheless, this still comes back to the question of what it is that determines that the people in the team are working well together and work in a way that benefits the organisation as a whole. This is how Jocelyn looks at it.

"You need to have the right people to achieve success. We have done all of this together, but the leadership is very important for us to have been able to do it in a successful way".

I think that the leadership has an unbelievable influence on organisations, that is partly why I have written this book. Whether you see leadership at the top, in the middle or the bottom of an organisation, it lays a foundation and conveys which beliefs and values matter. It is crucial for the entire organisation's culture. This is something that Kim sees when he looks back at his time as a student at the school.

"The teachers wouldn't have been the same without Pascal. His personality and ideas affect the whole school. He moves! The weaknesses at the school are things he does everything to minimise as much as possible. I admire him".

Pascal's ability to influence the whole organisation is not something that just Kim has seen; even Barbara has. My conclusion is that Pascal has a significant role in the school's successes and this is because he has the ability to get others to follow him in what he wants to create.

"He leads the way for many others. There are many who appreciate him", says Barbara.

I told Internationella Engelska Skolan's then CEO Ralph that I was writing a book about Pascal but that it was also about Management by Values (MBV). Based on this, I asked whether he had any reflections on how Pascal's leadership is based on values and what it meant for the school in Sundsvall.

"It is extremely important. Pascal personifies the company's values. He has our full mandate and confidence to lead from this. This has meant that he thinks that the job is fun".

In this book, you have gotten to follow a journey where Pascal has played an important role. He hasn't been directly involved in the writing and he hasn't known what I formulated from my side, but he has been an extremely valuable sounding board. The energy, honesty, clarity, will to improve, to participate and to manage, to question, to see the risks, accuracy and a fantastic ability to come to the core of a message are some things I have come to experience for some months. It was Pascal who in the end formulated a title for the book that I could feel satisfied with after many months of brooding. He is surely not completely happy with the title of the book and will continue to see the potential for improvement. I think that it has successfully caught the core of what I have chosen to talk about in this book. Every leader has a mandate to manage and lead. In this mandate, you must make sure that you yourself have enough knowledge to complete the task and to make choices. Leaders and organisations have a responsibility to use values as the engine of their success. To choose this type of leadership, courage is needed. Courage to gather an organisation around chosen values and stick to them. Courage to take time to build and uphold a culture that is built on values. Courage to encourage and speak up when employees move away from the values. Courage to, with current and future staff, decide on the right person in the right place. Courage to come back to what can be considered obvious or hokey to paint a picture and make it concrete. Courage to be a leader that is one with the company's beliefs, values, culture, mission and vision.

At the end of this book-writing process, I sent a summary to Pascal for opinions. Many in this situation may not really dare to say exactly what they are thinking, in consideration or cowardice, to not risk that I who has worked so hard over so many months would be upset. Pascal said himself he worried that he was perhaps a little too clear and honest. It is complex to write a story when it is about someone else. Of course, Pascal should recognise himself in my writing and feel that I quoted him correctly. At the same time, he doesn't need to agree with everything I think and have written. My image of him, the school and MBV is mine. Here I draw my picture as a contribution to a discussion about one of society's most important functions, leaders. Below is how Pascal expressed his expectations of the book in an email when I had just two chapters left to write, as usual he formulates himself in a way that is clear and successfully crystallises the most important part. He also shows what has been setting the tone for him during the whole project, that is, that the school is extremely important to him:

> I have understood that the book is about leading by knowing exactly what you stand for and the courage to implement it. I have also understood that the frustration you feel is about what you miss in other schools. What we have done well at IESS is that we have succeeded in getting a clear under-standing of what we stand for. You have expressed that through the word 'values'. We usually use the word 'ethos'. This has made it possible for us to build a strong feeling for what we want to achieve and that is what we are

What We Stand For

From the start in 1993, the founder, Mrs. Barbara Bergstrom, articulated three major convictions which still characterize Internationella Engelska Skolan:

Command of English. English has become the world's common language, "the key to the world". Children should learn to command the English language, not just know it, at an early age. Fluency is best achieved through language immersion, instructed by native English-speaking teachers in an international atmosphere.

A safe and orderly school environment where teachers can teach and students learn. Order, structure and safety are necessary prerequisites for learning. A school characterized by discipline and calm learning conditions also signals respect for the value of education. "Tough love" became the motto for a school which is strict in norms for behavior, but simultaneously conveys love for the students and a strong will to help each child succeed. Practicing good manners and proper behavior in a workplace combined with an appreciation of the positive results of hard work prepares students for success in adult life.

High academic expectations and aspirations. Our conviction is that every child can achieve success irrespective of social background. This ambition to support every student to realize his or her own potential applies to those requiring special support to meet standards as well as the most gifted learners.

Internationella Engelska Skolan is dedicated to supporting students of all backgrounds to become productive and responsible citizens, and to acquire the confidence and ambition to do the most with their talents.

engelska.se

FIGURE 15.3
"What We Believe In" has been referred to many times during the interviews for this book. This can be found at Internationella Engelska Skolan's website. Source: www.engelska.se. Internationella Engelska Skolan. What we stand for. https: //engelska.se/about-ies/what-we-stand (31 Auguist 2017).

going to build upon. Through this, we have been able to push ourselves at the school a lot as we haven't needed to put energy into worrying that staff go in different directions or that they feel lost. This is very important since this describes IESS as a workplace in a clear way. /Pascal Brisson.

See Figure 15.3.

It will be exciting to follow Internationella Engelska Skolan Sundsvall in the future. In Autumn 2018, the building project will be complete. From what the story tells, I can imagine there will be more expansions after that, this is surely not the last. Petra describes their future challenges and her view of Pascal's role in the future:

> It is partly new for us that we now have staff who have been with us a longer time and place new expectations on us. How do we keep the fire going? How do we work with staff who are very driven and must have the opportunity to take the next step? There will be other challenges in the future when we become a bigger school. Our success is built on us continuing to have many children and youths wanting to go to our school. We will be close to 130 staff and that means more relationships for Pascal to be responsible for, than when we started with 25. Additionally, he wants to see everyone. He needs to be another type of leader today than what he was in the beginning. But Pascal is good at taking care of the big things. He is perhaps needed more today than he was then

Petra concludes.

NOTE

1. Internationella Engelska Skolan Sundsvall. About the school. https://sundsvall.en gelska.se/about-our-school/our-story (07 August 2017).

16

Let's Round off This Conversation

When mistakes are made you help. When someone succeeds you tell the world.

Liza-Maria Norlin

How do I round this off? I don't know why you chose to read this book or what it is that you do that has brought you here or perhaps you have skipped to the last chapter. This book is a discussion about leadership. A kind of leadership that is needed today and something that will be the key to sustainable and successful organisations in the coming years. When I started writing this book, I didn't know where it would end. You have gotten to follow me on my journey and in my learning process that is built on curiosity, frustration and a will to be a part of and change things for the better. I want to increase interest in and the knowledge about values, and provide increased insight into their decisive meaning. If there is something that I want you to take with you from all the theories and examples that you have read, it is one of the first pictures in the book from *Managing by Values*. It describes what values are and how they arise and what consequences they have. Let me now explain the picture by using Internationella Engelska Skolan Sundsvall (IESS) as an example.

Let's say we are in agreement that it is one of Sweden's best schools and that is their *outcome*. If Barbara or Pascal had begun their leadership with this outcome as a starting point, they would have then had to go backwards in the model to successfully achieve the desired outcome, or maybe they would not have thought about this model without searching for organisational solutions to become one of the best schools. If you want to build an excellent organisation, it is not possible to copy Internationella Engelska Skolan (IES) or try to copy their culture and beliefs. The risk you take when your starting point is the outcome is that you aren't going to reach it exactly. I think that IES is successful as their founder had and has a *belief* that the ability to command the English language is important for every individual and that students can learn in an international and safe environment with high academic expectations. These beliefs were then formulated as values and became a part of the school's mission and vision. This also characterises all policies, guidelines and rules. Everyone in the organisation is expected to be one with these values. That is why the recruitment process for new employees is highly prioritised. All this lays the foundation for the school in Sundsvall together with Pascal's leadership and in one working community to create *norms* that lead to *attitudes*, and *behaviours* (culture) that are completely in line with the original belief. This becomes a strong engine and navigator that leads to the desired outcome, of it becoming successful. During all the years that the school has existed, they have learnt from their *experiences*, which develops the organisation and guarantees that they can refine from what has happened around them. This is a continuous apprenticeship with the beliefs and values as their starting point. See Figure 16.1.

My aim with this book was to write about values-driven leadership; I saw that Pascal represents just that. Sure, I am more convinced of that today while at the same time I see that leadership builds on what is basically a strong belief: "what they believe in". Of course Pascal wants to see results;

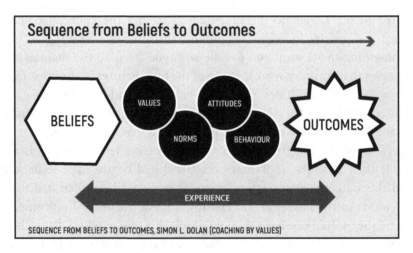

FIGURE 16.1

A model from *Coaching by Values* about the steps from beliefs to outcomes. Dolan, S. L. (2011). *Coaching by Values*. iUniverse, Page 87. Used with permission from Simon L. Dolan. Figure created by Norlins förlag.

he measures, evaluates and focuses on different goals but everything is always well anchored in the values.

> I agree with you on your analysis of Barbara. That is what I have tried to tell but haven't really been able to explain. What we have here in Sundsvall are beliefs that sometimes can lead to values that then lead to a clear identity. That identity and our continuous work for that identity makes us different from other schools

says Pascal.

"How is leadership connected to the work of building an identity?"

> Leadership in this case is about having courage to put time in talking about values, to implement them and to find strategies to communicate them. The values need to come from the leader, that doesn't mean that the leader as a person has exactly "the perfect values". Take for example Steve Jobs, he had clear values for his company but as a person, he had his issues. It's the same with me (smile) as with all leaders. Here the word values can be misunderstood.

"What do you mean with misunderstood?"

> For some, values can be being able to be a 'good person' and having strategies to be a good human being. Values can lead to this but they don't necessarily have to be good. Look for example at some extremist groups, they have clear values, values that are and could be dangerous. That is why it is important that the book makes the reader really understand the word values to avoid misunderstandings.

"How do you get the values to be clear and understandable in your leadership?"

> I always explain for my colleagues that the best way to "market" the school is to always talk about our beliefs. What we believe is more important than how we do something or why we do something. It is better expressed like this: "We believe that your child has the right to a safe environment so he or she can focus on his or her studies and can feel that he or she can be themself", rather than saying: "We have rules at the school that are…" or: "We have rules that make he or she feel safe". To communicate in that way, isn't actually about values but about beliefs.

When I talked to Simon the first time, he said to me: "Take everything you want and make it your own". The idea with management by values (MBV) is that it is built together through different experiences and contexts that are combined so that it can be developed as a method and concept. The word values is too big and broad a concept to stand on its own. That is why it is always defined and explained. I see this book as a beginning and an introduction to MBV and how you can coach through values. My hope is to be able to contribute to a deepened understanding for values and their importance for leadership. This is what Dolan says is needed to meet the challenges in our time: "Solving these problems will require both individual and group efforts, the efforts and cooperation of social organizations, government agencies, business leaders, the academic community and international organizations. At the core of these efforts must be healthy, sustainable values".[1]

As I wrote in the previous chapter, it was Pascal, who after many suggestions from me and others involved, that in the end suggested a title that I liked. This was suggested after he, without having read my book, defined what the book is about and I think he summarises it very well.

> The book is about leadership. Leadership for schools but not just for schools. A leadership that is built on knowing what you stand for and the courage to go through with it. The challenge with this kind of leadership is that everyone knows that it is important, everyone understands that, but there are still very few who are actually willing to put time and energy in delivering it. When you stand before the choice of efficiency or discussing values, most people choose the former. The book needs to get the reader to understand that. Yes, values and identity are important but it is very harmful if they are not implemented, as then they are just a difficult reminder of constant failure. Nothing is worse than if you have come to an agreement about values and they are then not implemented and complied with. So, to the title, I think it should and could be: "Courage to lead through values and identity".

"Great Pascal! Then it could be 'Courage to lead through values', identity can be what I write in my next book!"

Liza-Maria Norlin and Pascal Brisson are both available for lectures, seminars and workshops in both Sweden and abroad. Liza-Maria through her work as a politician, moderator, writer and teacher has extensively lectured about leadership. Pascal has been working in education since 1993 and as a school leader since December 2008. He has led workshops and lectures on Tough Meetings, Leadership and Engagement. To inquire please contact liza-maria@norlinsforlag.se

NOTE

1. Dolan, S. L. (2011). *Coaching by Values*. iUniverse, Page 79.

Definitions and Abbreviations

IES	Internationella Engelska Skolan
IESS	Internationella Engelska Skolan Sundsvall
Management by Values (MBV)	A management and leadership model that is built on the triaxial model. A method, theory and tool with values as a starting point. The creator of MBV is Simon L. Dolan.
Managing by values	In this book, this is used to refer to the book that Simon L. Dolan, Salvador Garcia and Bonnie Richley have written about MBV from a company perspective. Managing by Values is used by Dolan as well as a name for his method, theory and tool for values management.

Index